9/20

2 9 OCT 2022

CAERPHILLY
COUNTY BOROUGH COUNCIL
CAERFFILI
75 Tredegar Street
Risca
NP11 6BW
Tel: 01443 864780

Please return / renew this item by the last date shown above
Dychwelwch / Adnewyddwch erbyn y dyddiad olaf y nodir yma

A Champion Cyclist Against the Nazis

A Champion Cyclist Against the Nazis

Alberto Toscano

Pen & Sword
MILITARY
AN IMPRINT OF PEN & SWORD BOOKS LTD.
YORKSHIRE - PHILADELPHIA

Originally published in France as **Un Vélo contre la barbarie nazie. L'incroyable destin du champion Gino Bartali** by Alberto TOSCANO

© *Armand Colin, Malakoff, 2018*
ARMAND COLIN is a trademark of DUNOUD Editeur –
11, rue Paul Bert – 92240 Malakoff.

First published in Great Britain in 2020 by
Pen & Sword Military
An imprint of
Pen & Sword Books Ltd
Yorkshire - Philadelphia

ISBN 978 1 52675 339 7

Printed and bound in England
By TJ International Ltd.

Pen & Sword Books Ltd incorporates the Imprints of Pen & Sword Archaeology, Atlas, Aviation, Battleground, Discovery, Family History, History, Maritime, Military, Naval, Politics, Railways, Select, Transport, True Crime, Fiction, Frontline Books, Leo Cooper, Praetorian Press, Seaforth Publishing, Wharncliffe and White Owl.

For a complete list of Pen & Sword titles please contact

PEN & SWORD BOOKS LIMITED
47 Church Street, Barnsley, South Yorkshire, S70 2AS, England
E-mail: enquiries@pen-and-sword.co.uk
Website: www.pen-and-sword.co.uk

or

PEN AND SWORD BOOKS
1950 Lawrence Rd, Havertown, PA 19083, USA
E-mail: uspen-and-sword@casematepublishers.com
Website: www.penandswordbooks.com

To my mother, Ada, who was born the same year
as Bartali and who has traversed
a difficult century with optimism.

Contents

Preface – Gino the Just

Goodness has always fascinated me. Why, in a world where everyone turns in on themselves, where the instinct to die takes precedence over the impulse to live, why, when evil operated so openly during the time of Nazism, did certain men and women risk their lives to save others? Why? Why them and not other people?

Because those of us who fight for a little more solidarity among men, for a little more justice, need precedents, examples, fireflies in the darkness. This is the reason why, more than twenty years ago, I went in search of those Righteous whom, to allow the world to exist, the Talmud limits to 36, and Pascal to 4,000.

In Italy, where nearly 47,000 Jews lived in the early 1930s, about 7,000 were deported during the Second World War. And the others? They were spared or saved, despite fascism being in power. But by whom? And how?

In Florence, the city of Leonardo da Vinci, Dante and Michelangelo, the great American art historian and a specialist in the Italian Renaissance, Bernard Berenson, wrote from his Villa I Tatti where he lived, away from the Gestapo: 'Even a Dominican priest had to flee from his monastery for fear of being arrested and took refuge in my company'. Berenson also reported how the Cardinal of Florence, Elia Dalla Costa, declared himself to be guilty in place of a priest, whom the regime had accused of hiding a Jew. It was by following the story of this amazing and good man, who refused to open the windows of his rectory on the day of Hitler's visit to Florence, that I discovered the name of his friend, Gino Bartali.

What was this great champion of the cycling world, and one of the most-beloved sportsmen in Italy, doing in the same list as priests who had risked their lives to save others? I tried to reach out to him and ask him, with no result. I was informed that Gino Bartali had nothing to say as he had done nothing special. Apart from pedalling and winning cycling races.

My friend, Alberto Toscano, was luckier than me. He was probably more persevering. The story of sportsmen who opposed fascism fascinates him. The African-American athlete Jesse Owens, for example, who challenged Hitler, the cantor of the 'superior race' (white, of course), by winning the Berlin Summer Olympics in 1936. Or those who acted as true believers and true sportsmen, such as Gino Bartali, who took the Christian teaching of 'knock and the door will be opened to you' [Matthew 7:7] quite literally. 'Gino the Pious', who used his bike and his popularity to transport false papers throughout several Italian regions, thus opened the door of life to nearly 800 Italian Jews.

Alberto Toscano, a good, conscientious and precise journalist, has tracked down his hero. In this book, he describes how cycling, in a country where the sport remains the dream of several million teenagers, could pave the way for a champion, a sportsman no less admired by the Italians as his bicycle, to perform such a gesture of humanity.

One must read Alberto Toscano's text. It reads like an adventure and, moreover, restores a page that was missing from the ever-exciting and ever-present book of life.

Marek Halter

Introduction

There are times when sport makes history and there are athletes who win more than just medals. Hitler conceived the 1936 Olympics as the perfect stage for his racist propaganda and Jessie Owens showed the world the absurdity of racism. This book is about sport, history and politics. It examines the life of Gino Bartali, the man and the athlete, by sharing with him certain fundamental moments in Italian and European history. It talks about real events and uses authentic quotes, but Gino's life is so extraordinary that reality sometimes takes on an imaginary air and the truth can seem like a novel. This book is about an Italian who went through the twentieth century from beginning to end, becoming a protagonist in the life of his country. A simple and courageous man whose studies never extended beyond primary school, but who was always guided simply by respect for his values, his wisdom, and his will. He expressed it by doing what he knew and what he wanted to do: cycling. He engaged in sport, without refusing other obligations and without turning a blind eye to other problems or the problems of others. Politics while pedalling. The real politics. That of a logical person, not one with his head in the sand. When the events and tragedies of the Second World War put him in a dilemma, to make a stand or remain blind to the facts, Gino chose the first path and didn't hesitate to take risks in order to save lives.

Gino Bartali (1914–2000) is an exceedingly endearing character, and extremely attached to his homeland of Tuscany and his home city of Florence. It was here he experienced the two most difficult moments in the modern history of the Renaissance capital: the Nazi occupation of 1943–1944 and the devastation caused by the flooding of the Arno River in November 1966. As an athlete, Gino travelled more than 700,000 kilometres (435,000 miles) by bike: he could almost have gone to the Moon and back again, back to his beloved Florence. Along these 700,000 kilometres there are those who are interested in the history of sport and those who are interested in history.

Consider the first of these options. Bartali took part in 988 competitions and achieved 184 victories in the period 1931–1954. He won the Tour de France in 1938 and 1948 (twelve stage victories, twenty yellow jerseys, and two King of the Mountains jerseys: 1938 and 1948). He won the Giro d'Italia in 1936, 1937 and 1946 (seventeen stages, fifty pink jerseys, seven best climber awards: 1935, 1936, 1937, 1939, 1940, 1946, 1947). He also took part in four Milan – San Remo races (1939, 1940, 1947, 1950), two Tours of Switzerland (1946, 1947), three Tours of Lombardy (1936, 1939, 1940), three Tours of Piedmont (1937, 1939, 1951), five Tours of Tuscany (1939, 1940, 1948, 1950, 1953), a Tour de Romandie (1949), and a Tour of the Basque Country (1935). He was crowned champion of Italy four times (1935, 1937, 1940, 1952) and is described as one of the best 'climbers' of all time. Perhaps *the* best.

Yet in the outraged and martyred Italy of 1943-1944, Gino participated in another, very different, event. At the time, the country was divided in two, with the Allies advancing from the South against the German occupiers, supported by the fascists, who imposed their dominance and persecution over a large part of the country. Thousands of Jews hid themselves in shelters – some more safe than others. Many of them were refugees in convents. Although hidden, they needed forged identity papers in order to access food rations, to try to travel to a safer zone and, quite simply, so as not to be caught in the net of any raid. The network Gino was involved in was responsible for manufacturing and delivering these false documents. Indeed, it was for this purpose that the cycling champion travelled the most important kilometres of his life, and, in particular, the lives of others. Thousands of miles in the heart of a war-ravaged country, where every move provoked the suspicion of the Nazi-fascists and entailed enormous dangers. Bartali assumed these risks and it's thanks to courageous people like him that a clandestine network was able to save hundreds of Jews in Tuscany and Umbria.

When the war was over, Gino returned to his sporting activities. He never spoke, publicly, about what he did against the Nazi barbarism. He was just 'riding his bike'. We had to wait until the end of the century and the end of his life in order to filter precise information about his role in the network that provided aid to the persecuted, which had been very active in 1943-1944, especially in Florence and Assisi. Over the decades, books and films became more and more explicit about Bartali's role in the underground networks, which acted in coordination with the Italian Resistance. But Gino's attitude didn't change. He thought he had done his duty by helping to save lives. Nothing more. There was no reason to boast. Gino - nicknamed *Ginettaccio* thanks to his reputation for being an eternal grumbler and a 'kindly executioner' - never liked to talk about his activities outside the sport. He only wanted to be known and recognised for his achievements as a cyclist. He believed the other accolades would have eventually been awarded to him in another life and in another world.

I'm not able to know (and when I am able I won't be able to tell you ...) if, in the other world, Saint Peter gave him his medal. But we do know that after his death, the men of this world finally recognised all of his merits. In 2005, the Italian President Carlo Azeglio Ciampi, posthumously awarded Gino Bartali the 'gold medal for civic merit',[1] which he entrusted to his widow, Adriana, in 2006. The reasons given for the award were that, 'by collaborating with a clandestine network which hosted and assisted persecuted politicians and those who had escaped the Nazi-fascist raids in Tuscany, [Bartoli] had managed to save the lives of around 800 Jews'.[2] In 2013, the Yad Vashem Memorial in Jerusalem proclaimed

Gino Bartali as a 'Righteous Among the Nations'. This honour is attributed by the institution, after prolonged studies and detailed verification, to those non-Jews who acted with courage and at the risk of their own life in order to save the lives of several Jews, or even just the one, during the era of the Jewish genocide under the Nazis. The name of this cycling champion has become the symbol of his morality and a noble conception of sport: Gino always hated doping and carefully avoided any form of it. In trying to explain his philosophy to one of his three sons, Andrea, Gino once said very simply, 'I do not tolerate arrogance or those who practise it'.[3]

My own father sometimes spoke to me on the subject of arrogance suffered unjustly, although quite seldom, to tell the truth, about his personal experience. The experience of a man who, one morning in the Italian city of Novara, was dismissed from his work for 'racial reasons', having been dubbed a 'non-Aryan'. On 10 September 1943 he cycled to Lake Maggiore with the intention of taking refuge in Switzerland with his brother. On 12 September, German soldiers arrived in this area, which was close to the border. They had been on the Russian Front and so finishing the summer near Lake Maggiore had something of a holiday flavour for them. The hunt for migrants began. Rejected by the Swiss, the 36-year-old had to return to the Italian mountains and it was only at his second attempt that he finally managed to join the Swiss Confederation, which then forced him to stay in a refugee internment centre until the end of the war. Other people on the same route were captured and killed. In Meina, in the province of Novara, sixteen Jews were taken by the SS and shot on 15 September. Their bodies floated out on the waters of Lake Maggiore. A message and an omen.

I wanted to tell the reader that the writing of this book was something very special for me, and reminded me of the memory of stories heard long ago. The stories of a generation of people who have been through a terrible moment in European history. Those who attack Europe today should think about the memories of war that exist – or have existed – very much in the memory of their own family. This is certainly not a good reason to accept everything from Europe, but it is certainly a good reason to avoid destroying everything.

1. Italy: A Country that Pedals

In the beginning was the bike. 'You'll find your bike right now, or never,'[4] said the psychic to the unemployed Antonio Ricci, the protagonist of *Ladri di biciclette* (*Bicycle Thieves*). A beautiful film and a magnificent portrait of the poor and hardworking Italy of the immediate post-war period. A masterpiece of Italian neorealism, the film was released in 1948, the year when the sporting feat of one man - Gino Bartali's second victory in the Tour de France - symbolised the will of this same people to meet, to gather and to revive after the tragedies of fascism and war. The films [of this period] describing Italy stress the tragic dimension of the problem of unemployment in a society left to itself. Antonio Ricci is a father, unemployed for two years, for whom the 'bicycle' means 'hope'. You must pedal to change your life. With his wife and child he survives in a *borgata* (suburb) of Rome where, in this particular universe, former peasants find it difficult to become new workers. The setting is that of the suburbs invading the countryside, a concept that would be present in several films by Pier Paolo Pasolini, such as *Mamma Roma* (1962) and *Uccellacci e uccellini* (*The Hawks and the Sparrows*, 1966). Antonio Ricci, the hero of *Bicycle Thieves*, has the sensation of being reborn when he is offered work hanging posters around war-torn Rome. On one condition: he provides his own means of transportation. 'Ricci, don't forget to bring your bicycle'[5] says Antonio, in the Roman dialect, who is responsible for mediating between those who are unemployed and ready for anything, and the employers who are ready to exploit their distress. For Antonio, being without a bicycle means being without work and losing the much-needed opportunity to become a professional poster hanger.

In twentieth-century Italy, the bicycle was the horse of the poor, the peasant's horse, the horse of all those who had few resources and who had a (strong) desire to work. 'We were rural, peasant children',[6] Gino Bartali would say at the end of his life when speaking about his generation of cyclists. Simple, spontaneous and determined people, made of the same substance as their own dreams. And the first dream was simply to be able to eat properly. 'So I'd be able to eat something!'[7] said the peasant-cyclist Ottavio Bottecchia, in the dialect (sorry, language) of Friuli, when asked about competing in his first Tour de France in 1923.

The bicycle – or *bicicletta* in the language of Dante, who didn't have the chance to know one and therefore use it to go and sing serenades under the windows of his Beatrice – was the dream of generations of children looking for freedom. If the bicycle has so fascinated the Italians, it is because it is the son of their country and the father of desire and possibility. The desire to feel free like air, to move from one place to another, thanks to the muscles of a people used to pedalling. It especially meant the opportunity to work, in a country that (after the Second World War) was among the poorest and least organised in Western Europe. In the 1940s and 1950s, cycling practically rhymed with work.

The hopes of little Gino Bartali also took on the appearance of a bicycle. This time, it was about real life and not a neo-realist film. In twentieth-century Italy, cycling champions would turn the bicycle into a flag of national pride, as well as a symbol of work and freedom. To exalt this passion for cycling and the immense popularity of national champions on two wheels, the writer Curzio Malaparte described the irony and the paradox:

> *The bicycle in Italy is part of the national artistic heritage in the same way as the Mona Lisa, the dome of St. Peter or the Divine Comedy. It is surprising that it was not invented by Botticelli, Michelangelo or Raphael. If you happen to say, in Italy, that the bicycle was not invented by an Italian, you will see all eyes darken around you, a mask of sadness covering all faces.*

Malaparte writes these words in a little book that recalls, as described in his title, the Tuscan champion on two wheels: *The Two Faces of Italy: Coppi and Bartali* (1947), saying how the champions of cycling have become a true expression of the Italian nation and the faces of the 'Boot'.

As in the case of Giordano Cottur, the rider from Trieste who, in 1946 (at the centre of bitter international tensions following the Second World War) won in his home city one of the most dramatic stages in the history of the Giro d'Italia. Giordano raced for the *Wilier* team, which had been producing bikes in Bassano del Grappa, in Veneto, on the banks of the Brenta River, since 1906. At the time, Pietro Dal Molin, the company's boss, did not support the idea of Trieste being ceded to Tito's Yugoslavia. He turned his bicycles into 'rolling witnesses' of the national cause. He renamed his company *Wilier Triestina* and in the first edition of the Tour of Italy after the war (1946), made Giordano Cottur, a Trieste native, the leader of his team. In Trieste, the celebrations for Cottur became a signal to those participating in the Peace Conference to be held a few days later at the Palais du Luxembourg, in Paris, to define the Italian borders. Cottur's *Wilier Triestina* bicycle expressed Italy's desire for a revival on the occasion of the 1946 Giro, which was won overall by Gino Bartali. Today, in the twenty-first century, the Trieste cycle path, dedicated to Giordano Cottur, goes as far as Slovenia and therefore within the territory of the former Yugoslavia. A sign of peace in the shape of a bicycle, in the places where in 1945-1946, the very lively tensions of the post-war period in Europe existed.

Unfortunately for Malaparte, the best tribute to cycling is not the work of an Italian. However, do not be surprised. It's normal that the greatest artist of the twentieth century, Pablo Picasso, is also the author of the work that exalts the most exciting sport of that century, and the most profoundly human. I speak of the work which, in its extreme simplicity, is an apology for the bicycle by associating it with the fascination for the majestic animal that is the bull. And even – one can imagine – thus associating the bicycle with that fabulous creature of Greek mythology, the Minotaur. We want to think of a new Minotaur, with the head of a bull and the body of a bicycle. And to a new mythology adapted to the century that Gino Bartali had travelled through from beginning to end. Moreover, it is in his book *Mythologies* (1957) that Roland Barthes writes: 'There is an onomastic Tour de France that tells us on its own that the Tour is a great epic'. It's Barthes who compares the Tour to the Odyssey, making the cycling champion a Ulysses of modern times. As for Pablo Picasso, the work in question is, of course, the 'Bull's Head' sculpture made in 1942. The elemental and therefore natural combination of a bicycle's handlebars and a leather saddle to suggest a bull's head, throws us into a world of strength, determination and courage. The courage of Gino Bartali, who had been cycling since childhood and who became a global symbol of the sport. What's more, the bicycle reminds each of us of our childhood years and of family life. 'Alberto, don't go far when you play with your bike!' my mother used to say to me in Galliate, in the middle of rice and cornfields. The bicycle was that too. The most beautiful toy of my childhood. And perhaps that of yours, too.

For Gino Bartali, cycling was a complete member of his own family. He even slept with his bicycle, which he carefully kept in his room. Like other great cycling champions (Eddy Merckx and Marco Pantani, for example), he loved cleaning his own bike himself (with great care) after every race and every training ride. Gino spoke *to* his bicycle and much later he would talk *about* his bicycle, saying:

> *I was a nit-picker about everything when it came to my bike. When I was in the saddle, we were one. Not a weird noise, nor a misplaced screw could escape me. I took care of it myself. The only thing you could hear when I was riding was the light breeze in the bike's spokes and the air that it moved as it went along. How I cared about my bike! It was my companion, my life, my instrument of work.*[8]

In November 1940, Gino married Adriana, the cashier and shop assistant of a shop in Florence, to whom he had been engaged for four years. Adriana now received her first shock as she watched, stunned, the ceremony of Gino's return after a training ride. He began by having a bath, before immersing his adored bicycle, which he cleaned with loving care in the search for perfection, and with loving caresses. He washed it, cleaned it and pampered it as if it were a baby. A long time later, Adriana would tell her children that one day, Gino was walking along the streets of Florence holding her hand in one of his, and the handlebars of his bicycle in the other. With a smile, Adriana asked him: 'Which of us do you prefer?' To which Gino replied: 'You, of course!' Although his gaze appeared to turn to the bicycle as if to apologise, asking for its understanding and forgiveness. As if to explain to it that he couldn't answer otherwise. Much later, he would make a very unusual confession to Italian media: 'I looked at my bicycle like a lover!' Gino loved both his bike and his family. During the war, it was on a bicycle that on the night of 2-3 October 1941, he violated the curfew in Florence to fetch a midwife, before carrying her on the bicycleframe to his house so that she could take care of Adriana, who gave birth to their first son, Andrea. He would repeat this same mad race on the roads of Florence in 1943, in the desperate search for a doctor who, this time, would arrive too late: his child was stillborn. The next morning, Gino took the bike to bring the small body to the cemetery of Ponte a Ema, in the little coffin he'd made himself, and bury it in the family vault, right next to that of his brother, Giulio. A solitary funeral in the middle of the war. A man on a bicycle, in tears, with the body of a child who had never lived, who had never cried.

Today, many of Gino's bicycles are on display at the Bartali Museum. Where? In Florence, of course. In the suburban locality that is still Ponte a Ema, where the city dissolves into the countryside and hills.

Gino Bartali exaggerated a little, but it is also true that – for all those who were children – the bicycle is an object like no other. Those who don't like cycling are probably very unhappy people. Besides, along with an autographed photograph, the bicycle was the object Bartali brought as a gift to the Jewish boy Giorgio Goldenberg, on 16 July 1941, after he'd been driven from his school in Fiume because of fascist racial persecution, and who was now a refugee with his family in Fiesole, near Florence. This Jewish child had plenty of reasons to feel in danger, but Gino Bartali's little bike helped him dream of freedom. To always dream, and to cultivate the hope of a better world.

2. The Small World of Ponte a Ema

Gino was born in a suburb of Florence, in Ponte a Ema, where the Tuscan capital begins to dissolve into a horizon of hills drawn like embroidery. Indeed, Gino's mother, 'Mamma Giulia', could often be found embroidering during her free time, along with her two daughters, Anita and Natalina. In a region where craftsmanship was predominant, the needle and hook were a decent means of income. It could have been a currency in thousands of Italian villages, where home- and family-based craftsmanship was added (and added even more) to work carried out in the fields or in small factories.

Times were hard at the beginning of the twentieth century, and you had to find money in order to eat and to live. Spade in hand, Torello Bartali, Gino's father, would break his back in construction and agricultural work. In Italian, his profession was a *sterratore* (navvy, manual labourer); he moved the earth using nothing more than the strength of his arms. His dreams were simple: for his daughters to be married and to own a little piece of land that – one day, hopefully – his boys could work without being exploited. He believed in socialist ideals, so a little social justice would also be welcome.

Gino started working during his primary school years, helping his sisters make lace and spending part of his summer holiday in the raffia workshops. 'My dream was to have a bike', he would say much later in his memoirs. After six years at school, Gino left his studies with no regrets and began working as an apprentice mechanic for Oscar Casamonti, who owned a shop in the village that specialised in repairing bicycles. At the age of 12 he was able to achieve his first dream in life: with money from odd jobs and the family piggy bank, he was able to buy a used bicycle and although it was in very poor condition, he began repairing it with Casamonti. Thanks to the bike, he began to carry out errands for his family and neighbours. He didn't need to know Albert Einstein to discover the deeper meaning behind the physicist's famous saying: 'Life is like riding a bicycle: to keep your balance you must keep moving'. Gino earned a little money by delivering items, such as the fabrics that had been embroidered by the women in his family. There was, of course, a tram from Ponte a Ema to the centre of Florence, but he didn't need it. He had his bicycle. This extra work was an additional opportunity to pedal, pedal and pedal some more. The landscape of this part of Tuscany is ideal training ground for climbing and descending: beautiful to see and yet difficult to navigate when you're fuelled with bean soup and your bicep and quad muscles are your engine.

Ponte a Ema is part of the municipality of Florence, but at the time of Gino's birth it was still a traditional

Italian village, with its church, primary school and craft workshops. On 18 July 1914, in Florence as in the rest of Italy, the inhabitants thought of everything but the upcoming war. Newspapers talked of scandals, strikes and arguments in Parliament. The Balkans were far away and few people knew about a city named Sarajevo, where twenty days earlier, on 28 June, the young Bosnian Gavrilo Princip had assassinated the Archduke Franz Ferdinand of Habsburg and his lovely wife. The *Domenica del Corriere*, a weekly illustrated supplement of the daily *Il Corriere della Sera* newspaper, featured an image of the Sarajevo attack and devoted the last-page colour illustration to a violent dispute between Italian MPs, one of whom had overturned the box containing Parliament's ballot papers. Ten days after Gino's birth, the First World War began. A world war, but not yet an Italian one. The (very debatable) choice to enter into the conflict would be made by Rome the following year, on 26 April 1915, the same day of the secret agreement (the Treaty of London) between the Triple Entente (France, United Kingdom and Russia), and an Italy which was still theoretically allied with Berlin and Vienna. The Italian Parliament then voted to enter the war, but the decision had secretly already been made anyway. What was the point of voting? If that's the way it was to happen, then it's not surprising that the ballot boxes were thrown over!

On 24 May 1915 the Italians begin fighting along the border between Austro-Hungary and Italy (the Italian Front). Giulio, the last of the Bartali family, was born during the hostilities in 1916. The guns were a long way from Tuscany, but the dead came from all over Italy. Peace was declared in 1918, but the country was not peaceful. In three and a half years of horrific warfare, the country counted 650,000 dead, including 400,000 at the Front, 100,000 in captivity and 150,000 deaths or injuries from military operations. In this victorious and bruised Italy there were also 500,000 mutilated and disabled men. In addition, the Spanish Flu pandemic caused around 400,000 deaths between the end of 1918 and the beginning of 1919. The country was on the brink. The economic difficulties were enormous and society was torn apart, with neither the politicians nor the institutions able to cope with the consequences of opening 'Pandora's box' in 1915. In this context of crisis and confusion, the nationalist extreme right asserted its power through violence and on 28 October 1922, its leader was appointed President of the Council by King Victor Emmanuel III. The man in question, Benito Mussolini, was so-called because his father took advantage of his son's birth to pay homage to his left-wing ideals and the Mexican revolutionary, Benito Juarez. Bartali's father also leaned toward the left politically, but he certainly didn't want a revolution, be it Mexican or Italian. The Bartalis were a good Christian family who plodded along, one step after another, with the old and immortal wisdom of peasant Italy.

Gino's physique was absolutely not that of an athlete's. He was not tall (1.71m/5'6ft) and his muscles were not visible, even to the point where his friends made fun of his apparent fragility. Gino's response was always the same: everything was perfectly formed for cycling and he spent hours pedalling away. The adolescent Gino talked about his sporting passion to his boss, Oscar Casamonti, at the workshop where he was employed three days a week as an apprentice mechanic. Oscar was also an amateur cyclist, the sport being very popular in Italy as a whole with many competitions organised at all levels. The prizes for first place were often quite meagre, but times were hard and winning was a good habit to get into. What's more, riding and training were fun. One day, Oscar, who was now fully aware of Gino's passion for cycling, decided to take him along with some friends for a 100km training ride. Oscar saw himself as something of a champion cyclist, accelerating as soon as there was a hill while the other cyclists lost contact with him one after the other. All except for the young boy he had hired, whom he saw as a good apprentice mechanic, and who was now also beginning to look like a young champion in his beloved sport. Oscar had become almost a second father to Gino. His athletic father. The real baptism would take place on 19 July 1931, in Rovezzano (another suburb of Florence), during a cycling competition for boys under the age of 16. Gino won but was then disqualified as he'd celebrated his sixteenth birthday the day before the race, which was obviously reserved for 'under sixteens'. If only Mamma Giulia had waited a few hours before giving birth! Although Gino didn't win the big prize in Rovezzano, he did receive many compliments and, most importantly, he had tasted his first victory. That same year, he participated in eight races and won three.

But now there was a problem. Two, to be more precise. The first was the opposition of his father, Torello Bartali, to the idea that his son could choose the bicycle as a trade. It's interesting to imagine a conversation between Torello and Gino as they (in front of other members of the family) discuss cycling as profession. In the film *Gino Bartali, l'intramontabile* (*Bartali: The Iron Man*), made in 2006 by Alberto Negrin for Italian television, it went as follows:

Father: Gino, you want to be a cyclist? What kind of job is that?
Son: A sporting profession!
Father: And what will we live on?
Son: The winnings!
Father: And what if you don't win?
Son: I will!

Thanks to the support of the rest of his family, particularly his brother Giulio, who was also a lover of the sport and an amateur cyclist himself, Gino could now solve the first problem, and Papa Torello gave him the green light. However, in order to make money, he had to win races. But did he need to win them or could he lose them? This was the second, more intriguing, issue. After his first series of victories in 1931, the young Bartali understood that you could actually make a lot more money by coming second. This was an important detail in a family where one was always afraid of poverty, and where you were accustomed to paying attention to money, even little pennies. Indeed, such was his superiority that during races for young amateurs, after starting off in a breakaway with another competitor, he would sometimes receive a rather unusual proposal from the other rider: 'You give me the victory and I'll give you my bonus!' This was how he repeatedly pocketed first and second places, while the financial rewards soon became interesting. A day's work at Oscar Casamonti's workshop, a job Bartali continued to undertake three days a week, earned him 10 lire. Meanwhile, a victory brought in between 40 and 50 lire and second place between 30 and 40. When Gino returned home with 90 lire, the family could celebrate and life seemed more beautiful, even if none of its members was aware of Gino's little secret in his fight against poverty.

Gino's racing tally in 1932 amounted to eleven victories and seventeen second places out of thirty-nine races in total. Bartali was a member of Ponte a Ema's *Società Sportiva Aquila* (Eagle Sports Club), whose leaders were all very experienced. Ever since the invention of the bicycle, every race was full of cordial and sometimes secret arrangements. Certain smaller ploys were understandable, such as the common case of a breakaway rider aiming for the stage victory and another whose thoughts are purely focused on the general classification of a stage race. The former will put in a big effort throughout the day after getting the latter to promise to give up the sprint on the finish line. In other situations, the borders of morality and even those of decency are sometimes crossed. In young Gino's case, the fear of poverty often resulted in such arrangements being made between friends. They didn't last long, however, because in early 1930s Tuscany, the *Società Sportiva Aquila* were hungry for victories. They offered Bartali a deal: 'For each victory we'll double the bonus, but you have to do everything you can to win!' So the 50 lire now became 100. Everyone was happy and sport won the day.

In 1933, Gino took part in twenty-nine races and won sixteen. Another sixteen victories followed in 1934, but this year was also marked by Bartali's first serious accident in his sporting life. In Grosseto, Tuscany, he was fully committed in the sprint when he was seriously injured in a crash. During a very cold winter, at a time when no one would have dared to talk about global warming, Gino suffered serious breathing difficulties after spending too long playing in the snow with his friends from Ponte a Ema. His broad nose and hoarse voice would for ever remain two of his most characteristic and famous features, not to mention his gruff, and yet benevolent, personality, which earned him the untranslatable nickname of *Ginettaccio*. One of the Jews rescued by Bartali, Giorgio Goldenberg, would later say of him: 'He was a good man who forged a shell to protect himself'.[9]

Ginettaccio, the man with the generous, quibbling and grumbling nature, was one of Bartali's many nicknames; *Gino il Pio* (Gino the Pious, obviously due to his religious devotion), *Gino il Giusto* (Gino the Just, for his determination to always fight for those causes he deemed worthy of being defended) and *Gino il Vecchio* (Gino the Old, due to the longevity of his sporting career, which saw him competing for a quarter of a century). His other nicknames referred to his regional origins (the Tuscan Lion), to his fame as a climber (the King of the Mountains) and, as always, to his determination (the Iron Man). Yet the Iron Man had a heart of gold. Not just in terms of his compassion, but also medically: Bartali's heart was unusually strong and thus allowed him to achieve exceptional sporting performances. His resting heart rate averaged 32–34 beats per minute, which is quite a feat for a man weighing 64kg (10 stones) and measuring 1.71m (5′6). On 13 July 1937, the sports journalist Herman Grégoire published an article about Bartali in *Le Petit Parisien*, the leading French daily at the time, based on a conversation he had had with Eberardo Pavesi, the sports director of the Bartali's cycling team, *Legnano*. The article states: 'I met Pavesi, who was always tubbier, always balder, always friendlier than ever'. The journalist asked the man who had launched Bartali into the world of professional cycling what the secret was to his success. The reply? 'Bartali's secret? Let me tell you. Only when he makes an effort does his heart beat at the same pace as ours! Do you understand? His effort is what's normal for us!' However, Bartali's heart rate surprised some doctors, such was its peculiarity. During his medical examination when he was mobilised for the army in 1940, a military doctor even suggested he should be dismissed for health reasons. However, another doctor pointed out that it would be very unusual to dismiss someone on medical grounds after they had already won the Giro d'Italia and the Tour de France!

3. Gino the Pious

Gino Bartali always loved to define himself by his religious faith, which was so sincere, deep and so obviously displayed that it could sometimes seem a little naive. His faith accompanied him during races, with an icon of the Madonna hanging on his beloved bicycle. Bartali wouldn't be Bartali if he hadn't inherited a devout Christian belief from his mother, particularly in the fight against fascism. Indeed, this sporting champion would continue to refuse a PNF (National Fascist Party) card at a time when such an item was key to any career. When speaking about the Italian team at the 1937 Tour de France, he said: 'I was the only one not to have the fascist party card.' Unlike most other Italian athletes, he would also refuse to perform the *saluto romano* (fascist salute), and on the occasion of his victories, sometimes replaced this political worship with the sign of the cross instead. He would give thanks to God, rather than il Duce.

At the age of 10, Gino became a member of *Azione cattolica* (Catholic Action), a Roman Catholic lay association, keeping his membership card in his pocket and wearing a badge on his jacket for seventy-six years, until his last days. He might have changed his jacket, but never the badge. *Azione cattolica* was frequently and sometimes very intensely at odds with the Mussolini youth organisations (*Opera Nazionale Balilla, Gioventù italiana del Littorio*) and in general with the regime's institutions which were devoted to political indoctrination. Catholic and fascist youth organisations were often rivals, such as the FURCI (Italian Catholic Federation of University Students) who competed against the GUF (Fascist University Groups). Established in 1867, the *Azione cattolica*'s motto and agenda is three words: 'Prayer, action, sacrifice'. Bartali took these words very seriously, using them as his personal guide. He integrated prayer into his daily life, conceiving it as a moment of devotion, concentration and meditation. He attended Mass every morning, including (and especially) during major sporting competitions, such as the Giro d'Italia and the Tour de France. He rose at dawn, went to church and then made his way to the start of the stage – at that time, stages started earlier than they do today as they weren't designed around live TV broadcasts.

In 1936, at the age of 22, Gino Bartali was a well-known and nationally recognised champion. After his accident in 1934 he switched to becoming a professional cyclist, although he was unable to find a team willing to hire him. In 1935 he finally found a place in the Italian team, *Frejus*, which guaranteed him 300 lire per month, in addition to the bonuses that now no longer needed to be doubled. At this time, as it would be for decades, bicycle manufacturers were the driving force behind professional cycling, thanks to the teams that bore their names. Team *Frejus*, from

Turin, was consequently the first professional cycling team to hire Gino. In March 1935, the Milan – San Remo, the main 'classic' of Italian cycle racing, took place under Siberian conditions: of the 202 cyclists who set off, only 49 arrived at the finish line. Bartali was in the lead a dozen minutes or so from the end of the race, when the car belonging to the manager of the great Italian sports daily *La Gazzetta dello Sport*, came alongside him. The manager, the famous and influential Emilio Colombo, began speaking to him to try and distract him. Mostly, he wanted to make him talk, asking him questions about his life and his first sporting successes. The young Gino fell into the trap and, in slowing down, was joined by the famous Italian champion Learco Guerra (nicknamed the 'Human Locomotive') and his two chasing teammates. Gino learned an age-old lesson: 'Every flatterer lives at the expense of the one who listens to him'. A lesson worthy of a victory, no doubt. As Monsieur de La Fontaine would say, Bartali, 'shamefaced and in a troubled state, vowed to be tricked no more – a little late'.[10]

Shamefaced and in a troubled state, but still with two great satisfactions: a fourth place in the Milan – San Remo and an outsider role now recognised by the press, including that same newspaper which had 'tricked' him during the climbs in that part of Liguria, where the Apennines slide tenderly towards the Alps. This was a good thing, as *La Gazzetta dello Sport* formed the basis of the organisation behind the Giro d'Italia. First staged in 1909, Gino would compete in his first Giro in

1935, bringing home a stage victory (his first success as a professional racer), the climbers' prize and seventh place in the overall classification. A few months later, he was hired by a much larger team, *Legnano*, next to the legendary, but somewhat declining team, *Learco Guerra*. Pavesi, the team's *directeur sportif* (head coach), was to become not only Bartali's sporting advisor, but also his friend and confident. In the *Legnano* colours (green), Gino Bartali won his first big stage race, the Giro d'Italia on 7 June 1936, in Milan. It was his consecration. His happiness.

Sometimes extremes can touch each other and the line between great happiness and great misfortune becomes blurred, slippery, and almost non-existent. 'On 14 June 1936, the most terrible event of my whole life took place',[11] Bartali would say a long time later. During a race for young amateurs in Tuscany, his little brother Giulio, who was also a promising cyclist, collided head-on with a car that (in violation of all the rules) was driving in the opposite direction to the race. It was pouring with rain, the road was wet, and Giulio was unable to avoid the terrible collision. However, doctors at the hospital in Florence may have been able to prevent his death, but mistakes made by the surgeon were to prove fatal. At the time, Gino was competing in a race in Piedmont. He returned to Florence and sat by his little brother's bedside, holding his hand, before he died on 16 July. Gino was heartbroken. He also felt guilty and partly responsible for the tragedy that was engulfing his family. Giulio had looked up to his big brother and dreamed of following in his footsteps, both in life as well as on his lonely rides out on the Tuscan hills. For his part, Gino was proud of Giulio's admiration and thought that, as a racer, his little brother would have been able to imitate his success. When Giulio died, Gino stopped racing. Indeed, he stopped everything: shutting himself up in his house in Ponte a Ema, consumed by his pain and despair. In just ten days he had gone from his triumph at the Giro to deciding to give up cycling altogether. But when his fiancée Adriana went to see him at the family home, it was a bicycle she put in his hands, telling him, 'You have to race for him! Be yourself! You need to be the man and the rider that I fell in love with!' She achieved the desired effect: Gino got back on his bicycle and never left it again, just as he would never leave Adriana.

Yet it was not just love that led to Gino's decision to believe in life more than ever. In that incredible month of June 1936, comfort also came from his Christianity, giving him the feeling of being animated by a faith capable of giving meaning even to the most absurd and painful events. Life and death were two faces of a single mystery, which Gino tried to accept thanks to the strength of his convictions. His saw his future in the Christian religion and was particularly seduced by the spirituality of the Carmelites. In February 1937, he entered the Carmelite Third Order and would remain a member his entire life – even after death his body would be dressed according to the order's customs. Bartali was particularly devoted to the memory of the Carmelite nun, Saint Thérèse of

Lisieux, whom he called Saint Thérèse of the Child Jesus. He also, confidentially and tenderly, referred to her as 'Teresina' (little Thérèse) or 'Santa Teresina', considering her as a friend and not just his guardian angel. Saint Thérèse had entered the convent at the age of 15, just after praying for the most famous criminal of the time, Henri Pranzini (who was born in Egypt to a family of Italian emigrants and later settled in France), to convert before his execution. Today, the wax copy of Prizini's moustachioed and smiling face is on display at the *Musée de la Police*, in Paris's 5th arrondissement (he was convicted for the rue Montaigne triple murder in Paris and guillotined in 1887, aged 30). Thérèse died in Lisieux in 1897 at the age of 24. She was declared saint by Pope Pius XI in 1925 and Bartali was deeply affected by her life. He built a small chapel dedicated to his favourite saint in his apartment in Florence. (In 1997, Pope John-Paul II elevated Saint Thérèse to the rank of 'Doctor of the Church'.)[12] The champion of Ponte a Ema celebrated his victories by invoking the spirit of the Virgin Mary and Saint Thérèse of Lisieux. It was an act of faith, but also a challenge to the contemporary dictatorship: there were no words said for Benito Mussolini.

His devotion to Saint Thérèse significantly increased Gino's popularity in France. Since the spring of 1936, the country had been run by the Popular Front, but many people, even on the left, felt a certain tenderness for the memory of the girl who had wanted to save criminals from Hell, even if they were unable to save them from the guillotine. On 12 July 1937, *Le Petit Parisien*, which had a print run of over a million copies at the time, wrote: 'Ever since French Catholics learned of Bartali's special devotion to the little sister of Lisieux, there are as many letters from France in his mailbox as there are from Italy.'

In July 1937 France welcomed the Vatican Secretary of State, Cardinal Eugenio Pacelli (the future Pope Pius XII), who arrived from Rome as a papal legate to attend the ceremonies in Lisieux in honour of Saint Thérèse. The front page of *Le Matin* on 11 July declared: 'Lisieux celebrates the arrival of cardinal Pacelli'. In its issue of 17 July, the great French weekly *L'Illustration* covered the event with a photograph of Cardinal Pacelli, accompanied by the words: 'The Lisieux Festival: The Pontifical Legate delivers his speech in front of the basilica he has just inaugurated'. The crowds in Lisieux were immense. As we will see later, Bartali, who at the time was racing in the Tour de France in the Alps, declared that he wanted to finish the race in order to return to the north of France and take this opportunity to travel to Lisieux.

4. Cycling, Fascism and Anti-fascism

In June 1924 Italy trembled following the assassination of Giacomo Matteotti, a socialist politician and leader of the party opposed to fascism. France, meanwhile, was applauding a bricklayer from Friuli, in north-east Italy, who had become a cycling champion: Ottavio Bottecchia. He had been awarded a bronze medal for valour during the First World War (he was part of a cycling battalion, naturally) and on 22 June 1924 he won the first stage of the Tour de France, from Paris to Le Havre. After winning the yellow jersey on the first day, he held on to it until the end of the race four weeks later, becoming the first champion to achieve this feat and the first Italian to win the Tour (although he'd made his name in the race the previous year, after finishing in second place). The French public took him to their hearts, and on the roads of France the people called him *Botescià*, morphing his Italian name so as to sound more French.

On 21 July 1924, the day after his triumphant arrival in Paris, *Le Journal* newspaper declared Bottecchia a son of the Tour, writing on its front page: 'Almost an unknown last year, even in his own country, where he was sacrificed to the great transalpine stars of the road, he has made his breakthrough in the Tour de France and covered himself in glory'. People were fascinated by this character, who was to become a legend of the Tour for his climbing abilities. His exploits on the Col d'Aubisque and the Col du Tourmalet were unforgettable.

The journey from the Great War to the Tour de France had been a difficult one for the 'bricklayer from Friuli', as this courageous young man, born in 1894 in San Martino (a province of Treviso), was called. Taken prisoner by the Austrians in late October 1917 during the Battle of Caporetto (the worst defeat in Italian military history), he was able to escape by bicycle to resume the fight against the Austro-German forces. Bottecchia came from a very poor family, but the memory of being hungry is often what fuels a cycling champion. *Botescià* saw the bicycle as his way up in the world. His great opportunity. He was also known as 'the carter' or 'the woodcutter of Friuli', referring to the other trades he had practised to earn money. In the days following the assassination of socialist leader Matteotti, the anti-fascist Bottecchia could not have imagined that three years later, it would be his turn to die – most probably murdered – in conditions that could be seen as reminiscent of the death of democracy in Italy.

Italy was trembling in June 1924 because fascism was gaining momentum. The dictatorship was beginning to show its true face, twenty months after the *Marcia su Roma* (March on Rome), when the far-right, led by Benito Mussolini, seized power 28 October 1922. On the afternoon of 10 June 1924, the leader of the socialist party, Giacomo Matteotti, left his home in the centre of Rome to walk to the Palazzo Montecitorio.[13] He wanted to persuade his fellow MPs to denounce the nascent fascist dictatorship, the corruption within the regime and the irregularities seen in recent elections. He would never reach Montecitorio. Abducted by members of the fascist political police, he was assassinated the same day, although his body would not be found until two months later. Italy was entering a long, dark totalitarian tunnel. It swept through the institutions and manifested itself in acts of brutality perpetrated by fascist gangs (*squadracce*), who were determined to silence any opposition to the regime throughout the country with threats and violence.

On the night of 3-4 October 1925, *squadracce* in Tuscany were ordered to 'cleanse' Florence in a series of attacks on left-wing activists. Among the victims was the former Socialist politician Gaetano Pilati, whom Gino's father, Torello Bartali, knew and admired for his courage and commitment to the less fortunate in society. Pilati had fought against Italy's intervention in the First World War, but had fought bravely when his time came, losing an arm in battle and earning the silver medal for valour. Pilati died on 7 October following the fascist attacks. Torello Bartali, himself a socialist, was filled with anxiety during this dramatic period in Florentine political life. His feelings would leave an impression on the young Gino, who was 11 at the time of Pilati's assassination and the attacks on other well-known activists.

Gino fettered about his father's concerns, but his imagination was taken over by the exploits of his idol, Ottavio Bottecchia, who went on to win the Tour in 1925. Bottecchia now finally had the money to buy a property in his home province and establish a small bicycle factory. His popularity, personal pride and his refusal to become an instrument of fascist propaganda disturbed the local representatives of the regime. On 3 June 1927 he was found seriously injured at the side of a road he often used during training rides, near his home in Friuli. After suffering twelve days of agony, Bottecchia died at the age of 32. Official sources said it was an accident, but no independent and serious investigation was carried out, while certain big names in cycling who were close to the regime were curiously absent at his funeral. Accusations of a political crime commissioned by a local fascist leader would take shape and become more and more credible over time, as revelations and subsequent journalistic investigations followed.

In 1924-1925 the fascist press tried to use Bottecchia's victories to its advantage, just as it did in 1936 with Bartali's. In both cases, however, the cycling champions maintained their democratic convictions. They raced, they won, but they avoided becoming pure and simple instruments of [fascist] official propaganda. This was an increasing concern for Mussolini, who in 1937 finally created an ad hoc ministry, the Ministry of Popular Culture, known to the Italians as *Minculpop* (perhaps with a certain irony judging by the curious sound of the acronym), which took over all propaganda and control of information from existing institutions. The *Minculpop* would send newspaper editors instructions of what to write and what articles to publish, an arrangement the Italians called *Minculpop velines*, as they reminded them of drawings reproduced on tissue paper from tracing images on window panes. These provisions were implicit in the case of Bottecchia and explicit for Bartali: do not talk about these two athletes for any reason other than sport. Bartali the man must be of no interest to the Italians. Indeed, the only press that did talk about Bartali as a person and not just a cyclist was the Catholic press.

As the Italian journalist and writer Gianni Mura says, Bartali was 'an exemplary anti-fascist'. He was never afraid to take risks. For example, one day in the autumn of 1937, while he was competing at the velodrome in Lyon, Mario Alessi, a communist political refugee who was also from Florence and whom Gino had known when he was very young, went to see him at his hotel to ask for help. He needed protection from the OVRA (*Organizzazione per la Vigilanza e la Repressione dell'Antifascismo*, the Italian fascist regime's secret police), who, with the aid of French far-right militants, were organising political assassinations on French soil. On 9 June 1937, in Bagnoles-de-l'Orne, a commando unit of hooded men murdered two Italian intellectuals, Carlo and Nello Rosselli, two brothers who had been political refugees in France and prominent opposers to Mussolini's rule. Bartali was aware of what had happened and found a solution for his childhood friend turned communist militant, using his connections to ensure that Alessi was looked after by Catholic circles in Lyon.

OVRA forced a sports journalist to make up a file on Bartali: the fascist secret service willingly used the media to spread 'fake news', discredit their opponents and also to incite violence. Bartali's file is still kept in the Italian archives in a folder under the name 'Ministry of the Interior. General Directorate of Public Security. Political Police Division'. It states that Bartali was 'intrinsically linked to Catholic Action' and that he 'considered himself to be a representative of Catholic youth and not of Fascism'.

Bartali (a man of faith, a sportsman and a man of peace) hated the bellicose rhetoric of fascism. He was an exemplary anti-fascist at a time when the symbiosis of sports and propaganda guaranteed success in all disciplines for those who accepted it, as well as an impressive array of personal benefits. To stay the course, Bartali was forced to give up many opportunities. Sport was seen by the regime as being a vital method of obtaining popular consensus, to the point that the Coni (the Italian National Olympic Committee) was placed under the control of the National Fascist Party (PNF). Fascism exalted the myths of 'Italianity' and 'race', whose sporting champions became, in spite of themselves, incarnations of the most brilliant examples of the county's citizens, and even political symbols, which could be put on show before both the national and international public. Bartali always tried to find the balance between sports and his refusal of political compromise. He was offered the party card, but refused. The same proposition was offered again several times, in a flattering and increasingly menacing tone. There was nothing to do. He refused again and again. The regime then tried to use him in any way it could: if Bartali would not perform the fascist salute, if he would not dress like a fascist (the famous black shirt), nor dedicate his victories to Mussolini, they had to find a way of connecting these same victories to the work of the founder of the so-called Italian empire. The headlines on the front pages of the national sports dailies very clearly expressed Mussolini's wishes and those of his party. It was always the same concept: Bartali the sportsman, yes; Bartali the man, no.

During the 1930s, *La Gazzetta dello Sport*, the main national sports newspaper and therefore the unofficial voice of the fascist government for all things sports orientated – including aviation, which fascinated public opinion at the time thanks to its achievements and records – made sure that Mussolini's ambitions were fulfilled. The paper increasely pressed home the idea of the link between sports and politics, making its readers believe that the real reasons behind the Italian champions' successes was not what was in their own heads, but what was in that of il Duce's. The newspaper's views (as well as that of other Italian media) did not take into account the personal opinions and feelings of athletes, who in most cases adapted to the circumstances. These sporting champions were now instruments of the regime and included such men as the footballer Giuseppe Meazza – who was not afraid of performing the *saluti romani* – the boxer Primo Carnera, the racing driver Tazio Nuvolari and the cyclists Learco Guerra, Alfredo Binda and even, despite his best efforts, Gino Bartali. *La Gazzetta dello Sport* described them as both products of fascism and as examples of the presumed Italian superiority. The paper's philosophy was summarised by the headline in the special edition of 16-17 August 1932, at the end of the Los Angeles Olympics: 'The X Olympiad has revealed and proved to the world the progress of Italian sport, which has been regenerated by fascism and the value of its Italian athletes'.[14]

The year before, when announcing the success of the first crossing of the Atlantic by a group of planes, *La Gazzetta dello Sport*'s headline on 7 January 1931 read: 'The wings of Fascist Italy under Balbo's command have earned the admiration of the world by defeating the Atlantic in a rapid and steady flight'.[15] Aviation at this time was somewhat of a competition, rather like the automobile. The pilots' exploits were likened to genuine sporting performances and fascist Italy paid great attention to them.

Meanwhile, victories at the Giro d'Italia were dedicated to Mussolini. This triumph guaranteed the winner the *Premio del Duce*, an award created so as to stamp the regime's brand on the most popular national cycling races. The seemingly endless headline that dominated *La Gazzetta* of 29 May 1933, at the end of the twenty-first edition of the Giro, was quite something: 'Binda, three-time world champion, brilliantly won the fifth victory in the Giro'd'Italia at the Arena finishing line, winning the first *Premio del Duce* and the first prize of the Party leadership'.[16] Phew!

The information was designed to prevent the reader from distinguishing between those sporting champions who were members of the Fascist Party, and those who were just doing their job and refusing to compromise their political values. On 8 June 1936, *La Gazzetta*'s headline read: 'Bartali triumphs in the 24th Giro d'Italia, winning his first *Premio del Duce*'.[17] A victory at the Giro established a sporting-political link, even if the winner would rather have thrown the prize into the water: something Bartali would do in the truest sense of the term in 1938, after his first success at the Tour de France, by throwing the medal given to him by Mussolini into the waters of the River Arno, in Florence.

5. The Tour de France

In 1937, which was also the year Baron Pierre de Coubertin[18] died, sport was undeniably used as a political weapon. Hitler had hosted the Olympics in Berlin the previous year and in 1937, Mussolini wanted more than anything for an Italian rider to win the Tour de France. Fascism was not a fan of cycling – it probably preferred football, motor racing or the very virile boxing – but the Tour de France was the Tour de France. Now, an Italian (perhaps only one) had the chance to win the most famous trophy in cycling: Gino Bartali. There was little doubt in Mussolini's mind that Bartali had to try to win, in the name of his home country. At that time, the Tour was raced by national teams and was thus a great political opportunity at a very significant moment in history. The link between Mussolini and France, which had been very strong during the First World War and had remained so until the autumn of 1935, suffered after the League of Nations placed economic sanctions against Italy following the 1935-1936 colonial war between Italy and Ethiopia (the sanctions were in force from November 1935 to July 1936). Mussolini's rapprochement with Hitler's Germany, evident in autumn 1936, took place in the context of the Italian controversy with the influential Franco-British contingent in Geneva, the seat of the League of Nations. In this political context, competitions featuring the two most popular sports (football and cycling) took on a special significance in 1937 and 1938.

In the spring of 1937, Bartali committed a serious act of carelessness by making a round trip from Florence to Milan by bicycle, although the more normal option would have been to travel by train. He pedalled for hundreds of kilometres, despite the rain and even a snowstorm. His reward didn't come in the shape of a medal, but rather bronchopneumonia and a high fever. Although he had wanted to use the journey to Milan as a form of training, he instead ended up in bed. The doctors were very worried, even at one stage fearing for his life. But, according to Bartali, [his brother] Giulio intervened from Heaven and protected him. After Gino recovered he began training again as if nothing had happened. He dominated the Giro d'Italia (winning overall victory as well as the best climber's award, four stage wins and managing sixteen days in the pink jersey), to the point that Italian newspapers urged him to take part in the Tour de France. One such paper was *Il Popolo d'Italia*, the daily newspaper established by Mussolini in autumn 1914, probably with the help of the French secret services, to persuade its readers to support Italian intervention in the First World War and which would later become the official newspaper of the Fascist party. It sent rather clear messages to Bartali: not going to the Tour would make him unworthy as an athlete and as an Italian. Worse, it was suggested that Bartali had demanded a lot of money to put his legs in the service of his country. The pressure was immense. This time, it was not a matter of simply being a member of a political party or not, but of defending his own reputation as a sporting champion and even his personal dignity. Gino decided to meet the challenge that had been practically imposed on him. He would regret it.

The beginning was exciting. On 8 July 1937, a photograph of Gino appeared on the front pages of French and Italian newspapers. *L'Humanité* wrote: 'In climbing the Galibier, Bartali has executed a dazzling performance'. The front page of *Le Matin* read: 'Today, the Galibier, with its 2,600 metre road through the ice, as well as its ice-cold rain proved the high value of the Italian champion, Bartali'. *Le Petit Parisien*, which declared in its subheading to be 'the most read newspaper in the whole world', wrote the following caption on its front page, under the photograph of the Florentine champion: 'The Galibier stage. The Italian Bartali wins and takes the yellow jersey from the German Bautz'. On the inside pages, Herman Grégoire, the special correspondent out on the Tour, wrote an article under the headline: 'Bartali? A grand master!' The following day, Gino had a serious accident: during the Grenoble – Briançon stage, he fell during a high-speed descent and ended up in the icy waters of the River Couleau.

Bartali described the accident to Herman Gregory himself, as well as the invaluable help he received from his teammate, Francesco Camusso:

> *Firstly, I felt myself thrown into the air, then I was choking: my face was in the water. I lifted my head, breathed, and when I saw my bike being carried away by the current, I grabbed it. I also saw my cap spinning in a whirlpool. That's when Camusso picked it up and pulled me out of there. He told me he had to leave and I answered that I had at least three broken ribs. I couldn't breathe. I thought I was cursed and would never get to Paris or Lisieux, or even to Pau so I could make a pilgrimage to Lourdes. But Camusso shouted: 'Come on, the bike isn't everything!' I didn't listen. 'Madonna! The Madonna!', I said, and suddenly, I didn't feel anything, there was no more pain: the icon I wore around my neck had protected me. The Madonna had saved me. I also had an icon on the bike. That was why it was still intact!*

Quite literally picked up by the Piedmontese Camusso, the Tuscan Bartali was able to resume the race and even keep the yellow jersey. Herman Grégoire's article in *Le Petit Parisien* of 9 July was entitled 'Bartali's Misery'. And the misery would still be there the next day, when his opponents attacked on the Col d'Izoard.[19] Gino lost 22 minutes and fell to sixth place overall. The competition was now open and in his *Le Petit Parisien* article on

11 July, under the headline 'Bartali heals his wounds', Herman Grégoire wrote:

> *I was able to get closer to Bartali, to understand him better and earn his trust. After listening to him, I felt a deep sympathy for him. I understood what he was missing and that like the ancient Romans, who took their homes and their gods wherever they went, he was suffering from having abandoned his friends and the little shine he had erected in his house in Florence.*

Grégoire was referring to the small private chapel at Bartali's house, dedicated to Saint Thérèse. Gino confided in him, explaining:

> *Last year, my brother Giulio, who raced as an amateur cyclist, was killed. I was very affected by his death and became depressed. I prayed more and was very keen to finish the race and go to Lisieux to see the little room where Saint Thérèse of the Child Jesus lived. I had pneumonia in the spring and didn't want to race in the Tour de France. I'm only twenty-three, I still have time, I only wanted to come to France if I was certain of victory. They told me that I wasn't a good Italian. I am a good Italian; I came and I did my best.*

> *Question from the journalist: And what are you going to do now, Bartali?*

> *Bartali's answer: I never said I wanted to give up!*

And yet the leaders of the Italian team forced Gino to withdraw. Mussolini didn't like to see his athletes suffering: they had to have muscles, not injuries, and so Bartali returned to Italy. It was said that if he hadn't done so, 'they' could have taken his passport away. Gino felt helpless, humiliated, and hurt, although more in pride than in any physical way. A clear idea had now formed in his head: return to France and win the Tour. *Vincere!* (Victory!) was the regime's number one motto. But Bartali wanted *vincere* for himself, and certainly not Mussolini.

Il Duce and his collaborators shared this view, but in their own way. In regards to the 1938 sporting year, Bartali was informed that a decision concerning his actions would be made for him: there would be no Giro d'Italia in 1938 and he must save his strength for the Tour de France. This meant he wouldn't be able to achieve something he was very eager to attempt: three consecutive victories at the Giro. That was that. Full stop. 'It is so willed where will and power are one, so ask no more!', says Dante Alighieri in his *Divine Comedy* (the Italian text has an extraordinary sound, which has made this passage one of the most famous of all national literature: *Vuolsi così colà dove si puote ciò che si vuole, e più non dimandare!*). Dante writes this in Hell and the regime's latest decision gives Gino the feeling of living in a new chapter of the infernal story. Gino must do as he was told, without further questions.

On the eve of the Tour, the city of Paris appeared to be the ideal setting for the triumph of Italian sport and a defence of fascism. On Sunday, 19 June 1938, the Italian football team won the World Cup, which was being held in France. The front page of *La Gazzetta dello Sport* on 20 June read: 'Apotheosis for fascist sport at the Stade de Paris. The Italian team's formidable victory at the Football World Championship'.[20] This idea of a fascist apotheosis (glorifying a subject to a divine level) was expressed by the article 'For the flag' (*'Per la bandiera'*), on the front page of a sports newspaper, according to which the champions 'raised their arms while performing the *saluo romano* in front of the presidential platform'. The journalist added: 'I couldn't avert my eyes from this image of their raised arms'. The members of the football team had presented themselves as genuine fascists and not as mere representatives of a country that happened to have a fascist government.

The difference between the two was no small matter. Some Italians were aware of this difference because (a few days after the footballers' defence of fascism) Gino Bartali triumphed when the Tour de France arrived at the Parc des Princes. However, despite the pressures that one can well imagine he was under, he refused to raise his arm in the *saluto romano*. There was no need to look for a gesture demonstrating Gino Bartali's personal political views at the Parc des Princes in Paris, or in *La Gazzetta dello Sport*, which on Monday, 1 August 1938, celebrated the Italian's triumph in the 32nd Tour de France. Gino the Pious did not raise his right arm, instead using it to do what the Italian press carefully avoided emphasising:

the sign of the cross, which at the time was an implicit challenge to Benito Mussolini's regime. Gino's attitude appealed to the French newspaper *La Croix*, which wrote on 2 August 1938: 'The best man undeniably won.' And even: 'It is normal for victory to reward a rider who possesses moral qualities, in addition to his exceptional physical abilities. Because Bartali is simple and straightforward, he accepts the victory at face value and is probably one of the few men who has put sport in its proper place.'

On the other hand, *La Gazzetta dello Sport*'s headlines on 1 August display the cryptic language typical of dictatorships. To begin with, there is an allusion to football: 'The relentless pace of fascist sport triumphs from one success to another'.[21] Sport can be called 'fascist', but not Bartali. After announcing his victory, where he had dominated the race winning by a margin of over eighteen minutes from the rider in second place and more than twenty-nine minutes from the rider in third, *La Gazzetta dello Sport* proudly announced that the Tuscan champion would receive the 'silver medal for athletic achievement' from Mussolini. It was this medal that Gino would throw into the Arno.

The French public, which booed the Italian footballers, applauded Bartali and his success. 'Bartali deserves his victory' wrote the socialist newspaper *Le Populaire*. According to *Le Petit Parisien*, he was 'the most dazzling climber ever known'. The *Intransigeant* said that during the last stage the riders were 'madly cheered all along the course, particularly Gino Bartali, the overall winner of the event'. This newspaper also paid tribute to the ex-racer Costante Girardengo, who had been the man Bartali had urgently wanted as the technical director of the Italian team in 1938. He had chosen him for his abilities, even though at the time Girardengo had led a rather solitary life.

Bartali's triumph in the Tour was also a very important source of joy for Italian migrants, including those who, despite their French passports, retained a nostalgia for their homeland. Men, women and children from the Italian peninsula waited for hours on the roads of the Alps, the Pyrenees and throughout the whole of France to see the man that all Italians abroad (maybe even more so than the Italians at home) saw as a positive symbol of the Italian people. The number of Italians in France was enormous, and those who had fled misery and dictatorship needed a moral figure to look up to. Bartali did his best to fulfil this task, representing the image of a noble and courageous Italy. It was exactly what Italian migrants needed. On 15 October 1938, *L'Illustration* published the article 'Foreigners in France' which said: 'By nationality, it is the Italians who are the most widely represented: 888 000, according to administrative data'. These people, who made important contributions to the development of France, came from all Italian regions. Sometimes they left to find work, sometimes to flee the fascist dictatorship and other times for both reasons. Bartali inspired all Italians in France and on 7 August 1938, the day after his victory in the Tour, a major Italian newspaper (*La Tribuna Illustrata*) featured a drawing on its front page showing Gino cycling down a French street and being applauded by a crowd of men, women and children. The caption said: 'Groups of compatriots from near and far throughout France climbed the mountains to encourage and cheer on Gino Bartali, who triumphantly passed by and dominated all his opponents'.[22] For once, the front page of *La Tribuna Illustrata* didn't include a single a word about fascism and Mussolini. There was simply the idea that Italians, especially those who had lived through the bitter experience of emigration, could come together and celebrate the achievements of an athlete and an admirable figure. The presence of many Italian émigrés in France at various stages of the Tour, who were there particularly to cheer on Bartali, would remain a constant in the sporting life of the cyclist. The French rider Raphaël Geminiani would say:

> *When Bartali was racing there were always hundreds of Italians who came to watch him. He was a god to them. When I saw him in the midst of those Italians who worshiped and celebrated him, I wondered how he could be so loved.*[23]

Gino's victory at the Tour was the last sporting firework of the summer of 1938, before an autumn full of political clouds rolled in.

Gino Bartali, winner of the 1938 Tour de France. (*Shutterstock*)

GINO BARTALI

VINCITORE DEI GIRI D'ITALIA 1936 & 1937
CAMPIONE D'ITALIA 1935–1937–1940
VINCITORE DEL TOUR DE FRANCE 1938

Signed photograph of Gino Bartali, dated 16 July 1941, to Giorgio Goldenberg, the Jewish child he would later hide in his cellar, along with other family members. Goldberg's crucial testimony to Yad Vashem earned the cycling champion the title of 'Righteous Among the Nations'. (*yadvashem.org*)

Gino Bartali and Jean Robic during the 1948 Tour de France. (*Shutterstock*)

Gino Bartali on his lap of honour after winning the Tour de France, 25 July 1948. (*akg-images/Interfoto/Foto*Wilhelm)

Gino Bartali during a stage of the Giro d'Italia in 1950. In the background, a young fan is seen wearing a coat. (*akg-images/Mondadori Portfolio/Angelo Cozzi*)

Gino Bartali and Orson Welles in conversation during the 1950 Tour de France. (*Wikicommons*)

Gino Bartali with his wife, Adriana, and two sons, Andrea and Luigi, at a cycling competition in the 1960s. (*akg-images/Mondadori Portfolio/Angelo Cozzi*)

6. The Race Laws

On 31 July 1938, the day Gino Bartali won the Tour de France, the Parisian daily newspaper *Le Journal* published an article about the tensions in Italy regarding the issue of race, a fascist expression that was enough, on its own, to show the racist escalation of Mussolini's regime. Even Pope Pius XI wanted to have his say: the Church, he believed, had the right and even the obligation to warn Italy's citizens against this drift towards anti-Semitism, the developments and consequences of which no one was able to foresee. At that time, the scourge of anti-Semitism was present throughout large parts of Europe (including France, the eldest daughter of the Church and the home of human rights). In Italy, however, using the model of what was happening in Hitler's Germany, the state was transforming this scourge into an ideological pillar, thus giving a legal cover to the discriminations as they made their official entry into law, and which would anticipate the monstrosities of the following years. In the Italy of 1938, racism became a 'state religion'.

Under the headline 'Mussolini responds to the pope's speech', the 31 July article read as follows:

The speech given by the pope yesterday at Castelgandolfo, to condemn racism, occupied about four columns of the Osservatore Romano[24], *the mouthpiece of the Holy See...Pius XI gave somewhat of a warning to fascism and deplored the fact that Italy was imitating Germany by adopting its racial policies.*

The accusation that upset Mussolini the most was not that of racism, but that of plagiarism. He considered his anti-Semitism as an entirely national product: authentic and individual. Certainly not the clone of the latest fashion to arrive from Germany. *Le Journal* reported il Duce's reply to Pius XI, the text of which testifies once more to the tensions that existed at the time between the Catholic Church and the fascist regime. To the crowd listening to one of his numerous speeches, Mussolini stated: 'Know and let everyone know that even in the matter of race, we will walk straight. To say that fascism has imitated someone or something is simply absurd'. The expression 'let everyone know' is very clear and its intended recipient easily identifiable: it was a respectable gentleman who dressed in white and usually lived on the other side of the Tiber.

While the latter is usually true, it is not always the case, and the pope does leave the Vatican to go to his summer residence in Castel Gandolfo, his summer residence in the hills around 23 km (14 miles) from Rome. In 1938 Pius XI went there a little earlier, on

2 May, after considering the air in Rome to have become unbreathable and unhealthy due to Hitler's imminent arrival in the Italian capital. The next day, 3 May, Hitler was welcomed by the king, il Duce and the population of the Eternal City with great pomp and ceremony. Pius XI left the Vatican on the eve of Hitler's arrival, while the *Osservatore Romano* described the pontif's journey with words that are easy to decipher: 'The pope has left for Castel Gandolfo. The air of Castelli Romani is very good for his health.'[25] The air in Rome had become harmful. To mark his bitterness, Pius XI decided to temporarily close the Vatican Museums and to turn off all night time illuminations within the Vatican City. The Rome of Mussolini was jubilant, while the flags in the Vatican flew at half-mast. The Vatican City was in a national state of mourning, although the fascist regime tried to obscure it and with some degree of success.

The national press (obviously) and the international press (unfortunately) didn't give the pope's response the political importance it deserved. To read the commentary today of Hitler's visit to Italy (to Rome, Naples and Florence) from 3 to 9 May 1938 leaves a bitter taste in the mouth. Is that just a coincidence? A naive fascination regarding the miraculous side of Rome's welcome to Hitler? Or is there something else behind the attitude of a large majority of the French press, which was impressed by the brilliance of Hitler's visit and remained rather ambivalent when it came to stressing Pope Pius XI's reaction? In his report from Rome, published in

L'Humanité on Wednesday, 4 May, Gabriel Péri wrote: 'On the eve of the Führer's arrival in Rome, on Monday evening to be exact, the Quai d'Orsay [location of the French Ministry of Foreign Affairs] urged the press not to write anything that might trouble Italian-German relations!' Mussolini's contacts with the French and the British were still intense at this time, as would be seen less than five months later, in Munich. The pope's attitude certainly worried Mussolini and Hitler, but not so Paris or London. The Catholic newspaper *La Croix* was therefore relatively isolated in showing its great interest in the Vatican's courageous actions.

On 4 May, *Le Petit Parisien* reported on the Eternal City's lavish welcome of Adolf Hitler: 'Rome has given the event its allure of glorification: the message here is universal'. While the headline in *Le Matin* described: 'A fairytale procession to the Quirinal Palace'. In contrast, *La Croix* strongly emphasised Pope Pius XI's critical attitude towards Hitler's visit. On the front page of the 4 May issue, the day after the Führer's arrival in Rome, *La Croix* talked about the 'war of the two crosses' that had now been 'declared' between both the symbols of Christianity and the Nazi Party, the latter of which it described as a 'caricature emblem'. On 8 May *La Croix*'s front page included the headline: 'Hitler in Rome – The accusing silence of *L'Osservatore romano* – The closed Vatican Museums'. For its part, the headline of *L'Intransigeant* on 7 May read: 'In Rome, in honour of the Führer – [A] Colossal parade of troops in the Avenue des

Triomphes'. 'A triumphant climax to an extraordinary week' began *Le Matin*'s report from Florence on 10 May, where Hitler, accompanied by Mussolini, had ended his Italian visit. It was a triumphant climax to a certain extent: the Cardinal of Florence, Elia Dalla Costa had ordered (in an obvious act of protest against the Führer's racism) to close the doors and windows of the archbishop's palace on the day Hitler and his cortège of 500 Nazi dignitaries visited the city. On the same day (10 May), *La Croix* published a report from Rome under the headline: 'The swastika in Rome – The Pope's protests'. It stated that 'the pontif's protest had made all the more of an impression and was even more accentuated, as no voice in the press had yet risen: it was like a thunderbolt in a universally silent sky'. Even the international free press was conditioned by the gigantic propaganda machine operated by the two dictators and the impressive setting of the visit to the Italian cities, not to mention the 'fairytale' staging (as described in *Le Petit Parisien*) of Hitler's visit to Rome.

The director Ettore Scola chose this 'fairytale' setting of the Führer's visit to tell a story that was anything but a fairy tale. It is a story of private individuals, in which he depicts the weight of discrimination in this explosive year. He showed us the very different and very real humiliations experienced by a homosexual journalist and a mother, beautifully portrayed by Marcello Mastroianni and Sophia Loren, respectively. The journalist, dismissed from his job on national radio, is arrested at the end of the film by the political police for being homosexual. At the same time, the regime decides to dismiss all Jewish journalists from the Italian media, whether public or private. The film *A Special Day*, was released in 1977 and is a genuine masterpiece of Italian cinema, showing on one hand the loneliness of a persecuted man, and on the other the seemingly majestic counterpart of a society ready to 'believe, obey, fight' according to the regime's slogan.

After persecuting those with a different political opinion, in 1938 Mussolini decided to attack those he regarded as being 'different' altogether, fabricating a new enemy within Italian society from scratch. The main victims of this institutionalised infernal machine were Jews, whose numbers in Italy at the time amounted to around 47,000 (later around 36,000 in 1943 and 28,000 in 1945). Other persecuted people must be added to these figures as, according to the fascists, even those families who hadn't practised the religion for many years, or no longer had contact with Jewish communities, were also considered to be Jewish. In addition, the presence of several thousand foreign Jews in Italy must also be taken into account. This meant the number of people at risk of racial persecution was higher than the number of Jews identified as such by the Italian communities.

Italian society experienced a dramatic change in 1938 and while many may not have wanted to see or live through such change, it was impossible to ignore the new racial laws. Thanks to the goodwill of certain citizens, clandestine networks to help the Jews would be set up five years later, in which Gino Bartali would actively participate. These Italians (of different origins, opinions and religions) were able to come together in the name of humanity to meet the challenges of fighting racism, with an efficiency commensurate with their courage.

In 1938, Mussolini's anti-Semitic policies penetrated into the daily life of families, schools and businesses. Anti-Semitism was now part of the air you breathed in Italy (which, as Pope Pius XI would say, was becoming more and more unhealthy). It profoundly affected society as a whole, as Italians were bombarded with speeches about 'race', while their papers would soon carry *Ariani* (Aryan) or *Non Ariani* (Non-Arynan) articles. In February, the names of Jews within the armed forces, the administration and in academia began to be recorded. This identification and registration was intensified and extended during the following months on Mussolini's orders, while the Ministry of the Interior carried out a detailed census of Jews – Italian and foreign, the latter being promised expulsion – and (for the same purpose) created the 'General Directorate for Demography and Race'. On 15 July 1938, the *Il Giornale d'Italia* newspaper published a document signed by 180 fascist scientists. It was called *the Manifesto of Race*, and is better known as the *Manifesto degli scienziati razzisti*. The text would be reproduced in the first issue of the magazine *Difesa della razza* (Defense of Race), which appeared from 5 August and the main focus pointes were as follows:

> *Human races exist. The notion of race is a purely biological concept. The population of present-day Italy is mostly of Aryan origin and its civilisation is Aryan. There is now a pure "Italian race". It is time for Italians to proclaim themselves racist. Jews do not belong to the Italian race.*[26]

Goodwill aside, the Italian press were fully behind Mussolini's anti-Semitic campaign and on 18 September, he publicly acknowledged the "racial question" in his address to the crowd that had gathered at the Piazza Unità d'Italia in Trieste:

> *In terms of domestic politics, the pressing news is the problem of race. It directly concerns the conquest of the empire, for history shows us that if empires are conquered by arms, they are preserved by prestige. It directly concerns the conquest of the empire, for history shows us that empires are conquered by weapons, but preserved by prestige. And for prestige, we need a clear, severe racial conscience, which establishes not only differences, but very clear superiorities. The Jewish problem is therefore an aspect of this phenomenon.*[27]

The reaction of the foreign press to the Italian dictator's speech was grim and strange. The main headlines were primarily concerned with the parts of the speech covering the explosive question of Czechoslovakia, the main issue of the time, which in the following days would be at the centre of the Munich conference between Hitler, Mussolini, Chamberlain and Daladier (29-30 September 1938). However, on 19 September, the Parisian newspaper *Le Matin* accompanied its articles on the Trieste speech with a box under the heading: 'The Israelites will not be persecuted', before proceeding to summarise il Duce's speech as follows: 'As for racism, the Jews of Italy do not have to fear persecution. They will simply be separated from the rest of the nation.' No comment. In another article in the same edition, this French newspaper (one of the most widely-read in France) provided excerpts from Mussolini's speech with subtitles written by the editorial staff. The section on racism was subtitled 'Italy's generous anti-Semitism'. *Le Journal* provided the heading, in quotation marks: 'World Hebraism [is] the enemy of fascism'. Meanwhile, *Le Temps* and *La Croix* (thankfully) emphasised Pope Pius XI's attacks on Mussolini and were very harsh about il Duce's anti-Semitic policies. *Le Populaire*, the central organ of the Socialist Party (SFIO), spoke of the racial problem (without quotation marks), as if a racial problem genuinely did exist in Italy, rather than a racist delusion created from fascism. The regime had obviously invented the term 'racial problem' in order to justify its persecutions. Unfortunately, however, the expression began to creep more and more into the current language of the media at the time, and even into those newspapers that had no sympathy for Mussolini. *Le Populaire* included the following text: 'Mussolini confirmed that on the subject of race, 'necessary solutions' would be brought in.'

Journalists at the French Socialist newspaper should have known what these 'necessary solutions' to which the dictator was referring in Trieste consisted of. Just two weeks earlier, on 5 September, the government approved the decree entitled *Provvedimenti per la difesa della razza nella scuola fascista* (Measures for the Defense of Race in the Fascist School). During the period from September to November 1938, a series of decrees (which would become known as the 'Racial Laws of Fascist Italy') were approved by the Government of Rome and signed for promulgation by King Victor Emmanuel III, with the aim of structuring Italy's racist policies. These texts would be modified several times and made stricter during the following months and years. Many other anti-Semitic laws and regulations would follow, making Italy an officially racist country.

It was a country where young Jewish children could no longer go to public school, and where Jewish teachers would lose their jobs, as did all Jewish employees in public administration, banking and insurance. A country where every employee who worked for a state-related agency, something very common in Italy at the time, could be expelled overnight. A country where a Jew could no longer own a business or real estate, or even work in welfare or charitable institutions. A country where a

Jewish lawyer or architect was excluded from professional orders and could only practise their profession for people of their own 'race'. A country where marriage between Jews and people of 'Aryan race' was forbidden. At the same time, the regime defined the 'biological criterion' as the basis for its racist discrimination, meaning the children of Jews would be persecuted as such even if they practised another religion and even if they had done so for a long time.

The dictatorship asked Italians to look at their fellow citizens with suspicion and sometimes with hatred. Italian society has never experienced such racism within its borders and now it had to adapt to it. Or refuse to adapt to it. Everyone had to make a choice, whether it be the man on the street, religious institutions, businesses, or clandestine opposition political parties. All were forced to think about the 'racial question', its consequences and what behaviour to adopt in response to the hate campaign demanded by il Duce. There were also many who chose to act as if nothing had happened, as well as those who chose to help the Jews (as and when they could), who were becoming increasingly isolated and being persecuted more and more in public. Among those who were forced to question the situation and its prospects in particular was naturally the Italian Jewish community. In regards to its members, it was even absurd to use the word 'integration': Italian Jews are often among the most Italian of Italians! Indeed, there is an important Jewish community in Rome that dates back to the first century. It was true that *ghetti* (ghettoes) and discrimination existed and that Jews had suffered throughout Europe, including Italy for centuries, but there had never been Italian pogroms. During the *Risorgimento* (the unification of Italy in the nineteenth century), the Jews (including Daniele Manin, the Italian patriot and statesman who was forced to leave Venice to escape the Austrians following his commitment to Italian unity) played an important role. During the First World War, Jews fought alongside other Italians. Among them was a young volunteer, a corporal who fought on the front line on the high plateau of Asiago, who died on 28 January 1918 when he was not yet 18 years old. He was the son of the Venetian Jewish intellectual Margherita Sarfatti, with whom Benito Mussolini had had one of his most intense, long-lasting and important relationships of his life. Perhaps it was even the most important relationship, as it started when they were both young socialists and ended while they were together under the flags of fascism. Mussolini himself must have known how ridiculous it was to say that Jewish Italians were not real Italians. Many Italians knew this and (in their heart and sometimes in their behaviour) they refused to accept the racist stereotypes that were now so dear to the regime.

The 'racial question' became a tool for allowing people to see the ability of every Italian to think for himself. It divided the nation and tore up society. A 1970 film, *Il Giardino dei Finzi Contini* (The Garden of the Finzi-Continis) by Vittorio De Sica and based on Giorgio Bassani's eponymous novel, shows us the shock provoked by the 'racial laws' of 1938, which materialised by a series of events that marginalised the members of a wealthy Jewish family in Ferrara. The film begins with Jews being excluded from the local tennis club, then being kicked out of school and, finally, the tragedy of deportation. The Finzi-Continis of Bassani's novel and De Sica's film obviously felt perfectly Italian.

This was also the case for Mrs Elvira Finzi, from Milan, with the difference that this time, it was not a novel or a film, but real life. In September 1938, this teacher (Italian, Jewish and fascist) addressed a letter to 'Al Duce del Fascismo', which is preserved today in the State Archives:

Although Jewish for many centuries and more, I am Italian. I am a widow. My husband was an infantry officer, who was wounded and decorated during the Great War. I have an only son, who is registered at the Polytechnic. I have been a well-regarded and admired elementary school teacher for twenty-six years. I am being removed from this role, which is indispensible to me and to my son as it provides him with the opportunity to study. Do you really believe that such a terrible amputation of our life as perfect Italians, in our Italy, deserves this? With faith still in you alone, yours obediently, Elvira Finzi.[28]

7. Sport, War and Marriage

On 5 September 1938, the same day as the decree for the 'Defense of Race in the Fascist School' act came into force, public attention in Italy was partly distracted by a sporting event taking place in the Netherlands: the World Road Cycling Championships. The Italian team could no longer be divided and competition between the Italian riders was obvious. Old and new grudges prevented the possibility of any team strategy and the Italians were consequently beaten. Humiliated. The fascist press, which never missed an opportunity to attack Bartali, accused him of having played '*perso*' ('solo', ie, not a team player) and presented him as the main reason for the nation's defeat. This was, of course, totally untrue, but the opportunity to weaken the image of the man who refused to tow the party line was too good to resist. It was a bitter end to the year following his triumph at the Tour de France, and he was even booed by the Italian public during competitions at the velodrome. His response to all this was to win races. In Milan, in front a booing and jeering crowd, he removed the yellow jersey that he often wore in memory of his French victory. It was a way of telling the spectators, who were so conditioned by the press and the pressures of the regime, that he didn't consider them worthy of appreciating his sporting achievements. After removing his yellow jersey, he won every race in front of that same audience at the Milan velodrome, who now had no choice but to applaud.

His programme for 1939 included the Milan – San Remo, the Giro d'Italia and the Tour de France. He won the Milan – San Remo for the first time, but he soon realised that as far as the others were concerned during that cursed year, sport was now a hostage of politics more than ever before. Bartali came second at the Giro behind Giovanni Valetti, from Piedmont. There were those among Gino's friends who would say he was the victim of a plot, but he would never be able to prove such a thing. If he lost, then it was the result of having no luck and the (legitimate) tactics of his main opponent's team. It was part of the sport. As for his dream of a second consecutive victory at the Tour de France, politics once again got in the way. The Italian and German governments prevented riders from their two countries from participating in the Tour, which ran from 10 to 30 July 1939. Shortly after, on 23 August, foreign ministers Molotov and Ribbentrop signed the Nazi-Soviet Pact, in Moscow, with its secret plan for the partition of Poland (which Hitler invaded on 1 September, causing the outbreak of the Second World War, and Stalin later invaded on 17 September).

Italy was neutral and Mussolini would hesitate to commit until the German victory on the French front was no longer in doubt. Meanwhile, the rest of Europe took up arms, while Italy continued to focus on sport.

In 1940 Bartali won his second Milan – San Remo and had ambitions to win the Giro d'Italia. However, during a descent of the Apennines on the Turin to Genoa stage, a dog ran out into the road right in front of him. Despite his injuries, Bartali insisted on continuing the race, but a mechanical problem caused him to drop further in the overall rankings, while one of his *Legnano* teammates now found himself in a good position to win the Giro. His name was Fausto Coppi, and he was crowned the winner on 9 June 1940, at the finish of the final stage in Milan. Gino loyally helped his teammate, but understood that he would become a formidable rival in the future: Coppi was younger than him and had energy to spare. Once again, Gino was bitter, and for the second consecutive year he had to content himself with only an honourable showing at the Giro.

The next day, 10 June 1940, everything changed. In the afternoon, Foreign Minister Galeazzo Ciano (Mussolini's son-in-law, who would order the former's execution in January 1944) notified the British and French ambassadors of Italy's declaration of war. The French ambassador, André François-Poncet, spoke to Ciano and used a sentence that has gone down in history, comparing the attitude of fascist Italy to 'a stab in the back' (a phrase also used by President Roosevelt, who said: 'the hand that held the dagger has struck it into the back of his neighbour'). Soon after, at 6 pm, it was Mussolini's turn to declare war on France and Britain, with the support of the Italian population who had been overdosed on propaganda. The dictator appeared on his usual balcony in Palazzo Venezia, Rome, in front of tens of thousands of people crying, 'War! War!' Similar crowds, and even similar cries appeared in all major Italian cities, where the speech was broadcast live on the radio and amplified so much by the speakers so dear to the regime that they threatened to burst people's eardrums. 'An hour, marked by destiny, echoes in the skies of our country. The time for irreversible decisions is here',[29] said Mussolini. His decisions would be irrevocable, ignoble and catastrophic indeed.

During the previous months, the Church in general and Catholic Action in particular had tried to oppose Italy's entry into the war. Bartali had tried to make his personal contribution to this generous, and largely useless, effort. As war began to enter into the lives of the Italian people, Bartali was heard to say: 'For a Catholic such as myself, the very idea of war was beastly'. What was all the more distressing was that it was a war against France, a country where he had many friends in the sporting world, as well as in the Church and Italian immigrants. It was an evil that immediately began to affect Italian families. Giorgio Bani, brother of Adriana Bani (Gino's fiancée), died on 28 June when the boat transporting soldiers between Italy and Albania (which was occupied by the Italians) exploded. There were 219 victims, officially, but there were probably many more as the exact number of soldiers onboard was unknown. The cause of the explosion is also unknown. Was it a mine, a torpedo or just an accident?

Adriana's shock was aggravated by the fact that Gino also had to swap his sports jersey for a uniform when he was assigned to a territorial unit, far from the front. Adriana was very depressed and before he left, Gino wanted to do all he could to make her feel better, so he offered to get married as soon as possible. He still had to leave, but would return for the wedding. This moment was not only fundamental for Gino's personal life, but also for his future moral and material commitment to the persecuted Jews. The couple already knew the Archbishop of Florence, Cardinal Elia Dalla Costa, and asked if he would officiate their wedding. Born in Veneto in 1872, the 68-year-old cardinal was very generous and open hearted and accepted the request. Gino also asked if he would bless the little chapel inside the couple's house in Florence, to which he agreed. They were married on 14 November 1940 in the chapel of the archdiocese, in Florence, and would remain together until Gino's death, sixty years later. After a short honeymoon, during which time the couple received a private audience with the new pontiff, Pius XII, Gino was assigned to another unit in Italy. His role was to act as a liaison between different units and he was given a motorcycle to carry out his task. However, he used his bicycle instead. Gino and Adriana's first child, a boy, was born on 3 October 1941 and named Andrea. Two more children, Luigi and Bianca Maria were born after the war. Adriana died in 2014, at the age of 95.

On 21 June 1941, Hitler attacked his former Soviet friends by launching Operation Barbarossa. In response, Mussolini decided to send Italian soldiers to fight with Germany against Stalin. It was a disaster. Italian forces found themselves in trouble everywhere, especially in North Africa. As for Italy itself, aerial warfare had meant that bombing had long been an issue for cities, roads and the country's railway lines. In addition, land war was soon about to arrive on Italian national soil. In November 1942, the Allies landed in Algeria and were set to jump into Sicily, which they did on 10 July 1943. Two weeks later, on 25 July, Mussolini was held accountable at the Grand Council of Fascism, which, in an atmosphere of extreme tension, held a vote of no confidence against him. The next day, il Duce was received by King Victor Emmanuel III, who had him arrested and transported to a police barracks and appointed Marshal Badoglio as the head of the government.

The Italian people, bruised by the war, welcomed the news of Mussolini's downfall with relief. Monuments dedicated to him throughout the country were pulled down and destroyed. But the fascist slogans written on walls and buildings were still there, and some are even still there in the twenty-first century, proof indeed that dictatorships are very effective when it comes to such propaganda, enforcing their ideas through indelible paint and military marches. They are also effective and formidable when it comes to producing files or records: if they are not destroyed in the aftermath of a change of political regime, then it means the change is not really complete. Such was the case for records of Italian Jews, which were compiled in great detail from 1938 by the services of the Ministry of the Interior and carefully preserved by the Directorate of Demography and Race. This meant the Germans could easily lay their hands on the detailed and intact files concerning Italian Jews. The Nazi invasion of Italy was approaching and persecution would soon go up a notch to a whole new level.

Marshal Pietro Badoglio (who had commanded the Italian army during the Ethiopian War of 1935-1936) became head of the government on 25 July. He stated that military operations would continue and that Italy was still allied with Germany. At the same time, Badoglio was secretly negotiating with the Allies, who were now present in the southern part of the country. On 3 September 1943, Italy signed the armistice with the Allies. However, it was not announced until 8 September, when General Dwight Eisenhower was broadcast on Radio Algiers, before being announced by Marshal Badoglio an hour later from Rome. The king and Badoglio did not stay in Rome for long, leaving for Brindisi, in Puglia, on 9 September and placing themselves under American protection. Meanwhile, the Italian armed forces, left without any orders from either the king or the government, were exposed to the arrogance and desire for revenge from the Germans, who quickly and massively strengthened their presence in the Italian peninsula with the intention of occupying it from north to south. German forces immediately set about disarming Italian military units present along the national borders (1,090,000 men) and in occupied areas in France, Yugoslavia and Greece (900,000 men). In an attempt to flee the Germans, part of the Italian military took refuge in the mountains, making an important contribution to the birth of the Resistance, which would later have a prominent political and military presence in Italy during the last stages of the war.

Nazis and fascists reorganised themselves. On 12 September 1943, a German commando unit under the command of SS Captain Otto Skorzeny (who would flee to Spain after the war and die there in 1975), freed Mussolini from captivity at Campo Imperatore, high in the Apennine mountains. Transported to Munich, il Duce met Hitler on 13 September to prepare for his return to Italy and the creation of the *Social Repubblica* (Rsi) (Italian Social Republic), also called the *Repubblica di Salò* (Salò Republic), named after the city in Lombardy, on Lake Garda, which would be the effective capital. The Rsi was created on 23 September and became the collaborationist pillar of the German dominance of the Italian peninsula (which was increasingly shrinking as the Allies pushed northwards) from summer 1943 to spring 1945. The collaborationists were engaged in fierce fighting against the Resistance and actively helped the Nazis in their hunt for Italian Jews. The Manifesto of Verona was approved by fascist representatives on 14 November 1943 and formed the ideological basis of the Rsi. It considered Italian Jews to be 'foreigners' who must be treated as enemies during the war and consequently interned, deported, neutralised and eliminated. In all, nearly 7,000 Italian Jews would be deported to Auschwitz and only a few hundred (including the chemist and writer Primo Levi, who would afterwards publish his memoirs under the title *Si c'est un homme* (If This is a Man)) would come back. If we add the numbers of those deported to other Nazi camps and those from foreign territories occupied by the Italians, around 8,000 Jews were sent to the death camps. It was an unspeakable tragedy. Fortunately, many Italian Jews (and those foreigners present in Italy) would survive thanks to escaping to other countries (particularly Switzerland) and especially thanks to the help of other Italians who were willing to hide them. Solidarity was not an empty word during this period, which was the most appalling in the history of reunified Italy.

The groups of Jews from northern cities who tried to flee to Switzerland in one way or another were continuously pursued by German units and collaborators, who were beginning to reorganise themselves once more. At the same time, Jews living in the area around Lake Orta and Lake Maggiore were arrested and killed, including Primo Levi's uncle and cousin. In all, fifty-seven Jews were murdered by the Germans in this part of Piedmont during the weeks following 8 September 1943. This dramatic period in Italian history is known as the Lake Maggiore Holocaust. Jews who arrived at the Swiss border were sometimes sent back to Italy by the Confederation's border guards, under the threat of being handed over to the Germans and collaborators. The Swiss closed-door policy didn't last forever and they did become more hospitable, even though many of the destitute and persecuted souls were placed in internment camps until the end of the war.

The most atrocious episode of anti-Semitic persecution in Italy, the raid on Rome's Jewish Quarter, took place during the first phase of the German invasion. It was where the Jews had lived for almost 2,000 years, and which the Italians called 'Judean place'. Today, in the area between the Portico of Octavia and the Synagogue, one can taste the typical gastronomy of the Roman Jews, starting with the famous 'Judean artichokes'. The raid took place on 16 October 1943, 'Black Saturday', and was the work of a Gestapo unit in collaboration with an SS unit, which had arrived especially from Germany. A total of 1,259 people were carried away in trucks. Following a summary check, 1,023 Roman Jews were arrested that day and deported to Auschwitz, plus one child who was born shortly after the arrest of his mother. Only 16 people would survive and none of the 200 children arrested and deported during the raid would be saved.

8. Secret Networks

Autumn 1943 saw the beginning of the Nazi-fascist hunt for Italian Jews, the aim of which was their extermination. Consequently, plans were soon developed to hide those being persecuted. Despite Pope Pius XII's silence following the roundup on 16 October and his general timidity in his speeches in relation to the anti-Semitic persecutions – all the more striking in comparison with the firm public attitude of his predecessor, Pius XI, who died on 10 February 1939 – several Italian Catholic figures began to organise themselves in order to avoid being arrested and deported. Pius XII was undoubtedly aware of these plans, which further complicates the historical debate surrounding his behaviour during this period.

At this time, the Church had the only independent network throughout the whole of Italy. However, for those Catholics who were engaged in the fight against the Nazi persecutions, extreme caution was needed as fascist ears were everywhere, and so those who took part in efforts to save the Jews had to stay in the shadows at all costs. Meanwhile, the politico-military resistance was coordinated and from September 1943 was also able to count on a clandestine capillary network, in addition to the armed units which benefited from military equipment being dropped from Allied planes. These *partigiani* (partisan) units operated mainly in the mountainous regions of the central and northern peninsula, where the sweeping operations of the occupiers and collaborators were more difficult to carry out successfully.

Despite being direct targets of persecution themselves, some members of the Italian Jewish community helped to organize their going into hiding, acting in coordination with Catholic figures and with the Resistance in order to combat the anti-Semitism and avoid being deported. Detailed plans could thus be transformed into a series of, sometimes very dynamic, protection networks, in addition to the thousands of efforts by ordinary people who were not part of any particular network, to hide Jews in apartments, cellars, attics and anywhere shelter could be found. This was the case for Armando (known as Armandino) Sizzi, Gino Bartali's cousin, who owned a bicycle shop in the centre of Florence, on via Pietrapiana. During a roundup, the two cousins saved a dozen people who were trying to flee by pushing them inside the shop and quickly closing the shutters. Two of the people, a Jew and a Gypsy, accepted Armandino's offer to hide in the shop's cellar for as long as possible. They would remain there until Florence was liberated by the Allies and the Italian Resistance in August 1944, following a terrible battle waged by the *Partigiani* in the streets and buildings of the devastated city.

Throughout the period 1943-1944 many Italians displayed extraordinary examples of solidarity and generosity. In what was a time of tragedy, many families harboured Jews at the risk of their own lives. But there were also informers, ready to sacrifice the lives of others thanks to hatred or greed. Gino Bartali hid the Goldenberg family, who (shortly after the introduction of the race laws in 1938) had initially fled the Adriatice town of Fiume (where they were a well-known Jewish family and had thus felt particularly threatened) for Fiesole, near Florence. When the danger increased following the arrival of the Germans, the Goldenberg parents and their two children sought a safer shelter. These Jews (who were friends of both Armando Sizzi and Gino) now found themselves at risk of deportation. The 11-year-old son, Giorgio Goldenberg, was placed in the Santa Marta Monastery in Settignano, near Florence, while father, mother and little Tea, 6, stayed with Gino before hiding in one of his cellars, which was naturally considered to be a more discreet hiding place. Mr Goldberg and Tea hardly ever left the cellar, while Mrs Goldberg only went out as little as possible. Gino made sure they had the minimum to survive (and unfortunately it was only the bare minimum), even during the very difficult period of 1943-1944. Aurelio Klein, a cousin of the Goldenbergs and likewise from Fiume, was hidden (and therefore saved) by Gino. During an interview with the Florentine newspaper *La Nazione* in 2005, Aurelio Klein said: 'Bartali offered them tangible aid. He did his own thing, knowing what he was doing.' He especially knew what he was risking.

The decision to help Jews was not isolated to Italy at this time. Hospitality sometimes only lasted a few days, other times several months. It was a solidarity that would be maintained until the end of hostilities, which, in Tuscany's case, was confirmed in the summer of 1944, when, one after another, the various cities of the region came under Allied control. Many Italians behaved exactly like Gino and Armandino: with courage and generosity. However, Bartali was a special case due to the multiple ways in which he participated in the formidable 'anti-deportation machine', driven by the personalities in the Catholic Church and the Jewish Community. This 'two religion network' was set up in September 1943, at the beginning of the German occupation, most notably in Liguria, Lombardy, Piedmont, Tuscany, Emilia-Romagna, Lazio and Umbria.

Certain places were of fundamental importance, especially big cities such as Florence, Rome and Genoa – home to one of the most important Italian Jewish communities as well as being a port city and therefore used to contact foreigners. Other important places for the networks were those steeped in history and populated by a dynamic and brave religious solidarity, such as Assisi in Umbria and Farneta, near Lucca, in Tuscany. The small town of Terontola, in Lazio, was also important due to its railway station.

The 'anti-deportation machine' was able to count on the commitment of several individuals in the Catholic Church, and in particular the Cardinal Archbishop of

Florence, Elia Dalla Costa. This was the same man who had dedicated Gino Bartali's small private chapel, officiated at his wedding to Adriana and baptised their child, as well as boycotting Hitler's visit to the Tuscan capital on 9 May 1938. There was also the Cardinal Archbishop of Genoa, Pietro Boetto, and the Bishop of Assisi, Giuseppe Placido Nicolini, although the bishops entrusted the direct contact with the various clandestine representatives of the Jewish community to some of their collaborators: Father Aldo Brunacci and Brother Rufino Niccacci in Assisi, Monsignor Francesco Repetto in Genoa and Father Leto Casini in Florence. Their names are all engraved on Yad Vashem's Wall of the Righteous, along with those of two other extraordinary characters who collaborated with the Italian anti-persecution network from Sweden and France. The Swedish consul in Genoa, Elow Kihlgren, was one of the contacts established by Monsignor Repetto, who had a direct relationship with the Apostolic Nuncio in Bern, Archbishop Filippo Bernardini, as well as working with Massimo Teglio, in Liguria, to hide Jews and try to load them onto boats in the Genoese harbour. Arrested by the Gestapo in the Ligurian capital in 1944, Elow Kihlgren was expelled from Italy but not before having experienced the hard life of Nazi prisons.

The Capuchin Franciscan friar Pierre-Marie Benoît was a Bible expert with a doctorate in philosophy. He was born Pierre Péteul in 1895 in Le Bourg-d'Iré (Maine-et-Loire) and in Italy was known as Padre Maria Benedetto.

He earned the nickname 'Father of the Jews' thanks to his (courageous and brilliant) actions to save those who risked deportation. During the first years of the war, when he was in Marseilles, he had already found a means of printing and delivering false passports for Jews (despite surveillance from both Vichy and the Germans), many of whom had subsequently been able to leave France by sea, or by going to Switzerland via the territories of the South-East, which were occupied by Italian forces from November 1942 to September 1943. Pierre-Marie Benoît arrived in Rome in July 1943, just before the fall of Mussolini, in order to speak to the Vatican about his plans to save the Jews. He remained in Rome and was still there when the general situation took a dramatic turn for the worse in September 1943, and the deportations and arrests had brought the Jewish community to its knees by the end of the year. Pierre-Marie Benoît took it upon himself to replace the leaders of this community and stand up to the racial persecution. When it came to defending the persecuted, he became somewhat more Jewish than the Jews themselves.

Benoît became one of the leaders of the Roman branch of DELASEM (Delegation for the Assistance of Jewish Emigrants; *Delegazione per l'assistenza degli emigranti*), many of whose members were forced to leave Italy or were arrested, deported, or killed. For those who were living in Rome under the occupation, life involved taking a thousand precautions in a situation of secrecy that made any operational task almost impossible. Thus it was that a

French Catholic monk became a key figure in the Italian Jewish network. DELASEM was created in December 1939 by the Ucei (Union of Jewish Communities in Italy; *Unione delle comunità ebraiche italiane*). Among its founding members were three very different characters, but who were all united by being persecuted themselves for being Jewish: Dante Almansi, the ex-fascist prefect and later president of the Ucei who had been excluded from serving in Italian public administration following the race laws; the Genoese lawyer Lelio Vittorio Valorba, vice-president of the Ucei and well-known in his city where he had, among other things, excellent relations with the archdiocese; and anti-fascist militant Raffaele Cantoni, who had links to the Italian resistance and was in contact with the Allies. An ex-fascist, a lawyer and an anti-fascist militant.

DELASEM was a legal organisation until September 1943, but its activities were forced to become clandestine after the German occupation of Italy and with the birth of the puppet state, *Repubblica social Italian*. Despite the existence of DELASEM, the Italian Jewish community would pay the price for its insufficient ability to understand the true nature and dimension of the dangers it faced. Even after the start of the German occupation, there were still those within the community who believed what they were being told by certain representatives of the occupying forces. On 26 September 1943 the Gestapo commander in Rome, Herbert Kappler, summoned the leader of the capital's Jewish community, Ugo Foà, and the president of the Ucei, Dante Almansi, and asked them to deliver 50 kilos of gold in 36 hours in exchange for the lives of the members of the local Jewish community. The gold was found with unprecedented speed and the treasure was delivered to Kappler within the scheduled time. However, it was not enough to prevent the roundup on 16 October 1943 and the deportation to Auschwitz of those Jews arrested during the raid.

DELASEM's initial objective – for which Raffaele Cantoni had been fighting for years – was to save, assist and help secure Jewish settlers arriving in Italy from Germany (including Austria) and from Eastern Europe. Some of those who arrived were completely helpless and had practically nothing, while others had a visa from a host country but had to find a way to get there. This was the situation in 1940 for Jews with a visa for Shanghai, which had been issued by the consul-general of the Republic of China in Vienna, Ho Feng-Shan (who would later be declared 'Righteous' in 2001 for saving 'hundreds, if not thousands' of Jews). Despite the changing situation in September 1943, DELASEM did not change its name, but rather its purpose. From now on it was a question of saving, hiding and, if possible, helping to evacuate Italian Jews (in addition to foreign Jews present in the country) to Switzerland or those areas of Italy that had already been liberated. This required a lot of money, which arrived in Genoa via Switzerland. Trustworthy individuals were then tasked with going to Genoa to collect the money and bring it to Florence and Rome, before the city was liberated on 4-5 June 1944 by General Mark W. Clark's American troops. During the period 1943-1944, DELASEM was consequently the primary means of assistance to the persecuted members of both large and small Jewish communities of Nazi-occupied Italy. It was the Jewish pillar of the great underground network, of which Gino Bartali was also a part.

Some Italian Jews played a key role in the 'anti-deportation machine'. In Genoa, many arrangements (such as the arrival of money from Switzerland and the clandestine departure of Jews in return) were managed by Massimo Teglio. A member of DELASEM, Teglio acted in cooperation with Riccardo Pacifici, the rabbi of Genoa, who was one of the first in the network to be arrested. He was sent to Auschwitz in 1943, along with his wife Wanda Abenaim, where they were both killed. The Jewish pillars of the Tuscan network were Giorgio Nissim, who was responsible for the towns along the coast (Lucca, Pisa and Livorno, where there were traditionally important Jewish communities) and then the whole region from December 1943, and Rabbi Nathan Cassuto, who was the main contact in Florence, where DELASEM met in Catholic buildings such as the sacristy of St Mark's Church. Rabbi Nathan Cassuto was well acquainted with Cardinal Elia Dalla Costa, the Archbishop of Florence, and their collaboration helped develop the project of hiding Jews in Tuscan convents. After being betrayed, Nathan Cassuto was arrested in Florence on 26 November 1943 while attending a meeting at Catholic Action's headquarters on

Via de' Pucci. Father Leto Casini was also at the meeting and would later resume his activities to help save the persecuted after spending time in prison.

Raffaele Cantoni was arrested in Florence three days later as he searched for information on Cassuto. He was accompanied by Anna Di Gioacchino (Cassuto's wife) and their friend Saul Campagnano. The fates of these individuals would be very different. Saul Campagnano died in Auschwitz in March 1944. Nathan Cassuto and Anna Cassuto Di Gioacchino were also deported to Auschwitz, but were separated on arrival. Nathan was then transferred to Gross-Rosen, where he died in February 1945, just before the camp was liberated. Anna was sent to Terezinstadt and was still there when it was liberated at the end of the war. She decided to live in Palestine, where she found work in a hospital, before being killed in an ambush on 13 April 1948 during the Arab-Israeli War. Raffaele Cantoni was in turn deported to Auschwitz, but never arrived there. On 6 December 1943, as his train bound for Poland crossed the Veneto towards Austria, Cantoni took advantage of a favourable situation and jumped off the train. He managed to reach Switzerland and made contact with a lawyer called Valobra, determined to continue his commitment to DELASEM. He also worked to establish a Jewish military unit (the 'Jewish Fighting Force'; *Chativah Yehudith Lochemeth*), who would fight as part of the British Army during the latter stages of the Italian Campaign.

Genoa and Florence were important locations for the new 'freeedom network', woven together by Catholic figures and the Jews of DELASEM. Valorba and Cantoni kept in touch from Switzerland with cardinals Boetto, Dalla Costa and Nicolini, who themselves were in close and constant contact with each other. Dalla Costa approached Gino Bartali at the beginning of autumn1943 about becoming a 'courier of freedom'. Emilio Berti, a great friend of Gino's, knew the cardinal well so accompanied him to the archbishop's palace. Dalla Costa talked about the benefits that the great sporting champion enjoyed. After all, Gino, aged 29 at the time, was a very famous sports star in Italy and was well-known by the occupiers. One day, a German column was stopped because two military cyclists, who were fans of the champion, recognised him and wanted more than anything to have the chance to talk with him. An autograph can save a life! Bartali had a perfectly plausible reason for riding his bike: he was training. The war would not last forever and it was reasonable to assume that, after the hostilities, sport would resume its place in the world. In short, he had to continue putting in the miles. The huge advantage for Gino was that he was able to move around at a time when it was unsafe for anyone to leave home, and travelling from one region to another involved risks, interrogations and searches.

After his marriage Gino Bartali led a relatively quiet military life, mainly thanks to his popularity, but also due to his unusual heart, which military doctors had considered an anomaly and so had decided to place him in territorial infantry units. The cycling champion was assigned to 'carry orders' for the army in Italy, which meant he could also participate in sporting events. Along with other figures from Italian sport, he took part in competitions that the regime hoped would give the population an almost impossible feeling of normality. Bartali had the opportunity to never be too far from his family. Before the fall of Mussolini on 25 July 1943, he was part of the 'road militia' (essentially the traffic police) and was based in Florence. On 8 September 1943 the armistice was announced and afterwards the substantial dissolution of the Italian Army – the day of *Tutti a casa*, literally 'Everybody Go Home', according to the title of the famous film directed by Luigi Comencini in 1960.

During the chaotic weeks during the summer of 1943, between 25 July and 8 September, a general arrived in Florence from Rome. According to Andrea Bartali's biography of his father (*Gino Bartali, mio papà*, p.75), he approached the members of the road militia about the possibility of him 'resigning'. Gino submitted his resignation and, again according to Andrea's account, was 'released from his military obligations'. However, he was only free to a certain extent as, once installed in power, the collaborationist authorities in Florence tried to force him back into the army in autumn 1943. Gino was summoned before the new leaders of the road militia, who threatened to charge him for 'desertion'. Unable to leave, he was held in custody in one of Florence's prisons. The situation became very tense, but he was eventually released – thanks to an officer who was seduced by his sporting exploits – and almost forgotten about by the army.

In the book *La mia storia* (My Story), Bartali's account of his life to the journalist Mario Pancera, Gino reiterated his request for resignation and – having finally been released from all military obligations – was able to return to live at home. In reality, it was not just his 'resignation' from the road militia that allowed Bartali to return finally to civilian life. The resignation itself was absolutely worthless to the new collaborationist authorities of the Republic of Salò and the two additional factors that helped him leave the army were the chaotic situation and (once again) the high status of his popularity. Whenever someone tried to create problems for him, there were (thankfully) always others there who would help him out. He could have decided to lead a relatively quiet life, avoiding the many dangers of the moment as much as possible, but instead he chose a completely different option. He decided to put himself at the service of a humanitarian cause by using the privileges that derived from his sporting popularity, and join the networks helping those being persecuted, even though it meant enormous risks. If he had not been Gino Bartali, then he would not have been able to take advantage of certain benefits. But at the same time, if he had not been Gino Bartali, he would not have put those advantages at the service of others.

9. Gino the Just

Between autumn 1943 and summer 1944, Gino Bartali lived with Adriana and their son Andrea either in Florence or in country houses near to the Tuscan capital. He changed homes in order to stay in the shadows and reduce the risk of being identified as much as possible. He also wanted to protect himself from the curious eyes of the enemies and their informers, as well as from the bombing from 'friendly' planes (the Americans and British particularly targeted railway stations). Civilian casualties were high: 215 were killed during a single bombing raid on Florence, in what was the first of a long series, on 25 September 1943. Consequently, Gino began his humanitarian missions 'riding' on his bike.

During his meeting with Gino, the Archbishop of Florence, Elia Dalla Costa, insisted that he was one of the few people who could successfully fulfil the mission of being a 'courier of freedom' and be able to carry and hide the false identity papers that were needed to save hundreds of human lives. Gino knew that the metal bars of his racing bike were hollow inside. He also knew how to disassemble and reassemble them at full speed. After all, he'd worked as a bicycle repairer and it was hardly a difficult task for him. He could remove the saddle and seat post, fill the seat tube and other usable parts with documents, put it all back together in a few moments and start pedalling as if nothing had happened. He had to consider the risks for himself and his family: if something happened to him, Adriana and little Andrea would be alone in the middle of the storm. But how many people would die if he refused the cardinal's offer? Dozens, maybe hundreds. Gino spent a night praying before he accepted. He would lead his fight against Nazi barbarism by cycling between the different towns of central and northern Italy. He pedalled for months, driven by the knowledge that he was doing his duty as a man and by the hope that no one would ever believe that papers were hidden inside the metal framework of his bicycle. He won the bet. None of the German and fascist soldiers who confronted him on the roads of an Italy devastated by war would have imagined the key to his secret. By grinding out thousands of miles, Gino would certainly do everything he could to be recognised as the Great Bartali. It was all part of his plan. As a champion road cyclist, he was able to use the excuse that he was training. He was easily recognisable and Italians everywhere knew what he looked like. What's more, on his travels he often wore a shirt with the name 'Bartali' written on it in very large lettering: if someone didn't recognise his face, then they'd be able to read his name.

The plan conceived by the 'network of the two religions' was now clear. Men, women and children who were at risk of deportation must – whether hiding in monasteries or in private homes – have false identities in order to avoid raids, be able to eat (thanks to ration cards) and, if possible, to get away from cities where they could be easily recognised. They needed them to dream as well. Dream of a journey to those areas of Italy that were already liberated. These men, women, and children were good Jewish Italians, but must now be able to present themselves as good 'Aryan' Italians. It was that or risk being deported to Auschwitz, which would have meant almost certain death.

Extraordinary people, such as Bartali, were needed to carry these false papers, but extraordinary men with courage and know-how were also needed to make them. Such was the case of printers Luigi and Trento Brizi, from Assisi. In autumn 1943, Friar Rufino Niccacci contacted a politically motivated and professional printer in the city of Umbria, whose name was Luigi Brizi. He hated the Nazi-fascists, but (until his meeting with Niccacci) had not known what to do to fight against them. Now he did. Month after month, false papers came out of his studio as if they were perfectly genuine. Real jewels of the most noble counterfeit and the fruits of the craftsman Luigi's experience, who was helped both day and night by his son Trento. Their identity cards were produced using a very particular set of raw materials: real photographs, false details and a combination of either genuine or false stamps, which had been stolen by officials who were also ready to put their lives on the line. Some at great cost. Claudio Lastrina, for example, stole official stamps from the prefecture of Genoa, where he was employed. Arrested by the Germans, he was shot in 1944, although his torturers were unable to obtain any information from him regarding the clandestine networks.

The written information on the Jews' new identity papers needed to be false, believable and, above all, impossible to verify. The documents must have theoretically been issued by the public administration of a southern Italian city which had already been liberated by the Allies. As a result, the Nazis and their collaborators would not be able to verify the information by a simple telephone call. The names on the new papers needed to be above suspicion, so any name identifiable as Jewish was Italianised, while keeping a certain assonance with the original, so as to limit the risk of confusion on the part of the person concerned. Such precautions were particularly necessary in the case of children, who were more likely to get their false name wrong. Giorgio Goldenberg, for example (the child hidden in the Settignano monastery and, at the end of the German occupation of Florence, in Gino Bartali's cellar where his sister and his parents were already living), received fake documents under the name of Giorgio Goldini. It's easy to imagine how many times adults would have told him that his name was now Goldini. In a similar fashion, the name Frankenthal was likely to metamorphose into Franchi, while the Baruch family was now called Bartoli. Viterbi, a family name with Jewish connotations, became Vitelli. Ditto for Finzi, which became Figuccia, Luzzatto became

Luciani, and Majonica was changed to Majorana. As for the Franckfurter family, it would from then on be known as the Franchini family.

On each trip, Bartali would often come across Nazi checkpoints, but he showed no signs of nervousness. He spoke to the military as genially as possible, especially as they sometimes questioned him more about his sporting achievements than for the reasons behind this 'training' in wartime. He told them about the 'famous stage' of the Tour de France, or the defeat at his first Milan – San Remo, when he was still too naive to be a true champion. If one of them touched his bike, he asked them to take care as each piece had been designed and fitted to ensure maximum performance and speed. You didn't play around with a high-end racing bike! During these conversations with the soldiers of the Wehrmacht or Mussolini's army, everything came together in one big melting pot: the genuine desire to talk about his sporting exploits and the even more genuine fear of fuelling doubts about the reasons behind his journeys. He had to be clever, just like during the Giro and Tour stages, when he pretended to be sick before unleashing himself in a furious assault on his opponents. Or when he showed up at the start of a race with a cigarette in his mouth, as if to challenge the other cyclists by exhibiting an almost insulting nonchalance regarding the situation. The other competitors at the stages of the two major cycling competitions learned the hard way that Gino was considered as an artist of a new form of *commedia dell'arte,* where comedy was applied to sport in order to achieve victory.

This time the comedy was applied to an ultra-secret mission. Bartali knew that he would probably be killed if the true nature of his rides through the midst of moving armies and martyred populations was discovered. Moreover, as well as suggesting he become a 'courier of freedom', Cardinal Dalla Costa asked him for a formal commitment to respect the absolute secrecy of his travels and his mission. It had to be kept secret from everyone, including his family and his wife. When leaving the family home on one of his missions, he would tell Adriana that he was going training because, as a cycling champion, he wanted 'to keep fit'. He may even visit an old friend during his 'training', and so there was no need to worry if he didn't come home that night. He calmly answered Adriana's questions and dispelled any doubt she had, telling her that everything was fine. He asked his wife to trust him and Adriana knew that Gino deserved her trust. There was obviously much that was unsaid between the two spouses, but, above all that, there was mutual trust: the raw material of any solid human relationship.

Bartali's 'training sessions' included visiting the monasteries that were hiding Jews. Some of these were in Assisi, where St Francis was born in 1181 and died in 1226. His message is a hymn to hope and optimism, encouraging people to open up to others and to the world around them, particularly towards nature, which is always a source of meditation. The future can also be inspiring. After all, the day will always return after the night, and the coming of the night does not mean the death of hope. St Francis' prayer is a song of joy addressed to the Lord:

Praised are you for the laugh of a child
Praised are you for the moment
Praised are you for the forgiveness given
Praised are you for the love found!

Praised are you for the bird's song
Praised are you for the coolness of the water
Praised are you for the rain and the wind
Praised are you for the evening that descends!

Praise also for the monks in the monasteries, and for their courage. Assisi was the terminus of Bartali's main route. There were monasteries everywhere, and Gino always had something to do, either speaking or listening to those who harboured Jewish children. Fortunately, Assisi was not a strategic cog in the context of ongoing military operations in central Italy. There were no important lines of communication, industries, or power plants, and although there were many monasteries, there were no barracks. As a result, the city became increasingly important as a place for humanitarian aid. The Allies preserved it from bombing, treating it as if it were a huge hospital. From September 1943 to June 1944 (the liberation of Umbria), Gino completed dozens of 'training sessions' by bike between Florence and Assisi, particularly visiting the Poor Clare convent in San Quirico.

After the death of the cycling champion in 2000, Adriana personally visited some of the monasteries and convents where her husband had been during the war, after lovingly lying to her about the reasons for his travels. She went to Assisi (by car) accompanied by the writer Paolo Alberati. In the documentary *Bartali, il campione e l'eroe* (Bartali, the champion and the hero), which aired on Italian public television, Alberati described the conversation between Adriana and Sister Alfonsina Santucci. The latter told Adriana that she had met her husband 'at least forty times' during the dark period of the Second World War. Forty times in thirty weeks. That's a lot of visits!

The monasteries in Assisi were not only used to house Jews. On the initiative of Bishop Giuseppe Placido Nicolini and his collaborators Aldo Brunacci and Rufino Niccacci, these spiritual centres in the Umbrian city were the hub of anti-persecution in central Italy. These included the monastery of San Damiano (St Damian), with Father Rufino Niccacci, that of San Quirico of the Poor Clares, with abbess Giuseppina Biviglia and Sister Alfonsina Santucci, as well as the convent run by the Stigmata Sisters, with Mother Superior Ermella Brandi. Each location received the papers (from the Brizi printing house) and delivered them, directly or indirectly, to Bartali, who would arrive by bicycle and who always displayed a courteous and quiet demeanour. 'He was very kind and sensitive, but he didn't speak with other people', remembered Sister Eleonora Bifarini. Gino hid the documents in his bike when he brought them to Florence, giving them in turn to the trusted people designated by Monseigneur Dalla Costa. At the same time, Gino would leave Father Niccacci (or people he trusted) the identity photographs of Jews living in the Tuscan monasteries. These were then used to create the false documents he would collect on his return visit. Occasionally, Gino would deliver, or try to deliver, the false identity documents directly to people who were being hidden by families in Tuscany. Giulia Donati Baquis, who was hiding in Lido di Camaiore, would tell Yad Vashem officials after Bartali's death that he had visited the home of the family who were sheltering her, but was unable to leave the documents due to a misunderstanding out of his control: the person who opened the door feared a trap and pushed him away without allowing him to deliver the false papers.

The Brizi printing house, the home of the highly-skilled craftsmen and trustworthy anti-fascists, was the key to Bartali's travels on the Florentine axis towards the South, and the city of St Francis. The journey itself was nearly 200 km (124 miles) and although the current road measures 172 km (107 miles), the situation at the time was very different and required several detours. Documentation concerning the activities of Bishop Giuseppe Placido Nicolini, Don Aldo Brunacci, Father Rufino Niccacci, the Brizi printing house, the Convent of the Poor Clares, the Monastery of San Damiano and the other religious centres during the Resistance, is today kept at the Museum of Memory in Assisi. A memory to rediscover.

It so happened that on the road from Florence to Assisi, Gino stopped at the train station in Terontola, near Lake Trasimeno. Such locations were important from the point of view of the Resistance and once again, Bartali made use of his popularity, mainly by creating confusion when trains entered the station. The railway station at Terontola is one of the most important in central Italy, being located at the crossroads between the line from North to South and that leading to Perugia, the capital of Umbria. The confusion made it easier for wanted people to pass through the gaps between the Nazi-fascist military personnel who carefully patrolled the strategic location. Gino tried to get to Terontola station when a train was approaching and his friend Leo Pipparelli was often at the station bistro, ready to play the comedy role by shouting upon his arrival: 'Bartali's here! Bartali's arrived!' as the crowd quickly gathered around the champion. The German soldiers were forced to watch as the flow of travellers and the small crowd clearly demonstrated its enthusiasm for the famous sportsman. Gino's popularity created confusion and the confusion helped those who were trying not to be noticed, whether they wanted to get off the train and blend into the countryside, or climb onto the train and leave. Afterwards, Gino would resume on his way, sometimes passing between the military roadblocks.

Besides, the Nazi-fascist checkpoints were not the only danger: American planes risked strafing anything that moved. Whenever he saw these hunters overhead, Bartali hid and prayed. Fortunately, he hid well and prayed even better, although he would later say to his son, Andrea: 'Those planes would start strafing and only afterwards would they go down to see what they had strafed!'

Once back in Florence after a day (or two) away, Bartali knew that Cardinal Dalla Costa's fellow collaborators would send his precious cargo carried within his bike to the monasteries. In the meantime, these same monasteries were never idle. The monks and nuns prayed, as they had done for many centuries, and worked, according to the Latin motto of Saint Bennedict: *ora and labora*. Food for the spirit and, even more so, food for the body, is indispensable, all produced thanks to the 100 per cent organic agricultural work. In the convents where Jews were hidden, prayer was rather peculiar. After all, the monasteries were true Catholic schools for people who, with few exceptions, had no intention of converting. The women, men and children in particular, 'only' needed to show they were good Christians in order to save their skin.

The Jewish children in the monasteries of Assisi, Settignano, Lucca and many other Italian towns, learned to memorise, in both Italian and Latin, the *Ave Maria* and the *Pater Noster*. The better they knew the prayers, the more learned they were and the more likely they were to present themselves as 'Aryans'. As has already been said – but is worth mentioning again – the racist criterion of the Nazi-fascists was not religious, but 'biological'; they persecuted a 'non-Aryan', even if he or she converted to Christianity. For them, it was the same thing: a person was 'biologically' Jewish, even if they believed in Jesus who, in any case, would also have ended up in Auschwitz according to Hitler and Mussolini: he was Jewish and circumcised, according to the Gospel. A good knowledge of prayers was not an absolute guarantee to evade deportation, but it could certainly help someone avoid it. Especially if they also had false papers with a name more Italian than Margherita pizza. For the boys, the risk of being checked for circumcision always remained. However, this operation, especially in the context of a convent, posed problems even for the Nazis. It was difficult to practise systematically and may even have seemed unnecessary if the children knew the Christian prayers and had the correct identity papers.

The importance of the 'courier' Bartali was therefore relatively mainstream, as it was with others (some known and others most probably unknown) who, in one way or another, were involved in this Resistance network. Thanks to the documents brought by Gino, a Jewish child might leave the convent with his mother, or with a woman posing as a member of his family, to go in search of a new life. From that moment, the real problem became that of not being recognised by people they had met in their previous life. Vengeance and blackmail were serious issues for those in hiding. Some families had accounts to settle with their neighbour and an anonymous letter might be enough to 'settle the score', by sending the grandson of the man who had insulted the cousin of an aunt to a camp in Germany or Poland. The cowardice of some, like the heroism of others, showed itself in the worst moments of a society in crisis.

In addition to the Florence (Assisi axis), Bartali's trips also took him to the north-west, to the cities of Lucca and Genoa. The distance from Florence to Genoa is 230 kilometers (143 miles). On the way there or back, Bartali stopped off in Lucca, where there were two monasteries which were very involved in the 'network of two religions'. At one of these was Father Arturo Paoli, who risked his life by helping the Resistance and by hiding Jews (he would also risk it much later by defying the military dictatorship in Argentina in the 1970s). He died in Lucca in 2015 at the age of 103, and was declared 'just among the nations' at Yad Vashem. Bartali brought false documents to Lucca for the Jews in Father Arturo Paoli's monastery: Paoli was working with Giorgio Nissim, the man now in charge of DELASEM in Tuscany following the deportation of Rabbi Nathan Cassuto. By taking thousands of precautions, Arturo Paoli and Giorgio Nissim found a simple and brilliant way of avoiding the traps of the Nazi-fascist intelligence services. They took five lire banknotes and cut them in half, with Paoli keeping his half at the convent and Nissim giving his half to the person who was to seek shelter with the monks. On presenting themselves at the monastery door, this person would hand over the piece of his five lire banknote to

Father Paoli, who would then only let them inside if he himself possessed the other half of the same note. Only Arturo Paoli would be able to shelter the person, certain in the knowledge that it was not a Nazi trap.

The other monastery in Lucca frequented by Bartali – once again to deliver identity photographs and false papers – was the Farneta Charterhouse: a particularly important location for the network. Father Antonio Costa was in charge here, although he would have a much shorter life than Arturo Paoli. Antonio Costa and the Farneta Charterhouse would be at the centre of an appalling event in September 1944, at a time when Gino Bartali was no longer able to visit as the front had divided Tuscany in two. Florence had now been liberated, but Lucca was still in Nazi hands and wouldn't be liberated until 5 September 1944. With the assistance of an informer, the Germans and their collaborators obtained information on the presence of Jews and Resistance members within the Carthusian monastery. During the night of 1-2 September, German soldiers from the 16th Panzergrenadier-Division 'Reichsführer SS' burst into the monastery before leaving in the morning with their prisoners: monks and the dozens of people they had been hiding. In the following days, twelve monks from the Farneta Charterhouse (including the prior of the community, the Swiss Martin Binz, and the Frenchman Adrien Companion) and at least thirty-two Jews or Resistance members who had been hiding in the monastery, were shot over various days and in different locations by the Nazis as they retreated north. Among these victims of Nazi barbarism was Father Antonio Costa. As a monk, he had taken the name Dom Gabriele-Maria and had been in charge of the charterhouse's administration. After being tortured, he was shot on 10 September alongside a fellow monk from Farnet, the Swiss Dom Pio Egger, at the age of 46. During his interrogations, the only words he spoke were in prayer. Antonio Costa, a friend of Bartali, had visited the cycling champion in Florence in 1943 and celebrated Mass in his private chapel.

In Genoa, Bartali was not limited to delivering or receiving documents and messages that were useful to the work of the underground network. He also had to collect US dollars and Swiss francs. Thanks to the international DELASEM network, money would arrive from the Swiss Confederation and would be very useful when it came to financing certain operations to protect Jews. Sometimes this might have involved renting an apartment far from the city of origin, where a Jewish family would otherwise have risked being recognised and denounced to the Germans in spite of its new identity. In other cases, money was needed to finance smugglers who helped Jews travel to Switzerland in the north, or to those areas already liberated by the Allies in southern Italy. Particularly active and especially interested in this money were the 'smugglers of Abruzzo', who had inherited the know-how of the local rebels (a mix between the more romantic Robin Hood and the, much more prosaic, image of outlaws themselves). The 'smugglers of Abruzzo', as they were called when they operated as smugglers from occupied Italy to that of liberated Italy, were very loyal and even had their own patron saints – who acted on their behalf without asking for a percentage of the dollars that Bartali transported from the archbishopric of Genoa to Florence and possibly to Assisi as well. In his book *Gino Bartali, mio papa*, Andrea Bartali says that in the area around Rivisondoli (in the province of L'Aquila, in the middle of the Abruzzo mountains) the cycling champion had to contact a monk 'who knew all the smugglers, of whom he was also their confessor'.

Shortly before the liberation of Florence, Bartali also risked falling into the hands of one of the cruellest and most bloody military units and paramilitary forces of Italian collaborationism in the service of Hitler. The group was called the 'Carità Gang', named after the fascist Mario Carità, who had terrorised Florence during the period 1943–1944 at the head of the Italian SS. Gino was arrested by the gang members at the end of July 1944 and questioned about his relationship with the bishops. The merest hint of him having helped the Resistance risked his execution. He was held at the Villa Triste, as the Carità headquarters were called. Indeed, in several Italian localities, Villa Triste was the nickname given by the population to places of detention and torture in 1943–1944. Carità's men, who controlled the postal service, intercepted a letter to Bartali from the Vatican, thanking him for the food he'd sent to those in need. Carità believed it was a coded message, which was plausible. Gino was scared and after the war would say:

> *The interrogation took place in the cellar in the presence of Major Carità and three other soldiers. It was a sinister, terror-inspiring place. Those who entered it didn't know what state they would leave it in. As they interrogated me in an inquisitive and arrogant tone, the major blasphemed constantly in order to offend and provoke me. On the table, I saw letters with the Vatican stamp.*[30]

Gino was scared, but held his nerve. Despite being threatened, they could find nothing against him and – thanks once again to the help of someone present at the interrogation who was a great admirer of his sporting performances – Gino was able to regain his freedom, after being on the verge of a summary execution. Carità let him go, telling him that he intended to summon him again, but he never had the time. In August 1944, the city of Florence finally found its long-awaited freedom.

But its freedom had come at a cost; conditions were particularly difficult and there were dramatic losses among the civilian population. Finally, on 11 August, the sound of the 'Martinella', the bell that had been used to announce wars and great events to Florentines since the Middle Ages, launched its message of hope and peace. Not to mention fight. The Germans had left the city centre, but the collaborators were still well-hidden and well-armed in the suburban hills. A group of forty-nine British soldiers found themselves trapped in a house, Villa Selva, near Ponte a Ema, unable to leave thanks to fascist snipers all around them. Bartali found a black shirt (the fascist uniform) and was thus able to reach the house, from where he safely directed the British out into the countryside so that they could finally reach the safe zone. The British soldiers were free, and so was Florence. But Bartali was threatened once more, this time by an isolated group of armed and excitable men claiming to belong to the Resistance, who accused him of being a collaborator. If these men had only known the truth...

The war in Italy officially ended on 25 April 1945, which would afterwards become the National Day of Liberation. Captured by Resistance units while trying to escape to Switzerland, Benito Mussolini was shot on 28 April. His body was hung upside down in Piazzale Loreto, Milan, along with those of his closest collaborators and that of his faithful mistress, Claretta Petacci, who had all wanted to die by his side. By chance, Bartali passed by at the same time. After witnessing the scene, all he could think about was the past and the future of his country. As the Latin proverb says, thus passes the glory of the world: *Sic transit gloria mundi*!

10. Gino the Old

Although the war was over, Bartali said nothing of his extraordinary humanitarian achievements. His mind was focussed on his growing family (his second child, Luigi, was born in 1946) and the resumption of cycling competitions, which were also a means of feeding his family. He was a little uneasy by the idea of having lost a good part of the most promising years of his sporting life. Cycling champions usually mature around 30 years of age and Gino celebrated his thirty-first birthday in July 1945. There were those who called him Gino the Old, especially as he was unable to escape the comparison with the other national champion on two wheels: Fausto Coppi. Five years his junior, Coppi had won the last edition of the Giro d'Italia in 1940 and had just won the very prestigious Milan – San Remo in 1946. The old man and the youngster. It was a very unpleasant cliché for Gino. In his autobiographical book *Tutto sbagliato, tutto da rifare* (Mondadori Publishing, Milan, 1979) Bartali uses words full of emotion to describe this moment of his career, saying: 'I had to start all over again. One thing comes to mind, the fact that a lot of people, friends or opponents, had started to call me *il vecchiaccio*[31] (a friendly and ironic pejorative of *vecchio*, meaning 'old'). In his other autobiographical work, *La mia storia*, he says on page 65: 'I could still demonstrate to the younger generation that I was not the grandfather you took out for a walk from time to time.'[32] His age was almost becoming an obsession!

The first big challenge for Gino the Old, who felt younger than ever, was also the first Giro d'Italia of the post-war period. In 1946, the Giro was the most important race in the world as there was no Tour de France that year (the last edition of the Tour had taken place in 1939 and would resume in 1947). Gino absolutely wanted to seize this opportunity to show that he still had plenty of energy. Gino and Fausto started their duel for the pink jersey in the first full year of peace after the war, when the whole of Italy dreamed of finally having a life in pink.

The year 1946 gave Italians and many Europeans (although unfortunately not all) the wonderful feeling of having found the path to peace and freedom. Italy had freed itself from Mussolini and his dictatorship. The world war, the colonial conflicts and the German invasion were just an old nightmare. The country was struggling through hard times, but it was still there. The prophecy of the German soldier in the film *Gino Bartali, l'intramontabile* (Bartali: The Iron Man) didn't come true. When checking Gino's papers during one of his secret missions, he told him: 'After the war there will be no more Giro d'Italia because there will be no more Italy'. However, Italy was still there in 1945 and the revival of the Giro in 1946 was proof of its desire to return to normality. It was also the Giro of rebirth: rarely had a sporting event had so many political, moral and, it could be said, historical meaning.

Internationally, Italy was still exiled and this also applied to sport and cycling in particular. Italian riders were not allowed to participate in competitions that took place on the soil of other European countries, with the exception of Switzerland. Bartali, Coppi and the others were victims of an absurd and grotesque boycott, intended to make democratic Italy pay for the responsibilities of the fascist dictatorship. As if the price already paid by the Italian democracy hadn't been high enough. At this moment in time, sport and politics were inseparable. During the summer of 1946, Italian newspapers combined information on the Giro, which began on 15 June and ended on 7 July, with information on the preparations for the long-awaited International Peace Conference, which would begin in Paris on 16 July at the Luxembourg Palace, the seat of the French Senate. At the end of the conference, Italy would sign the Treaty of Peace on 10 February 1947. The page had now been turned once and for all. Finally. Thanks in particular to the moral and political legacy of the Resistance, Rome could now return, with her head held high, to the international community (in which, to tell the truth, there were very few countries and people who had nothing to reproach themselves for).

Italy was now a republic. The Italian state was still there, but the Savoy dynasty, which had done so much harm via the actions of King Victor Emmanuel III, lost power. The revival of the Giro d'Italia, which started in Milan on 15 June 1946, was a window to the future. The country was in turmoil. The referendum of 2 June 1946 (a date that would later become an Italian national holiday) consecrated the victory of the Republic against the discredited monarchy of Savoy. At the same time, the country voted for its Constituent Assembly, with the text of the Republican Constitution coming into force on 1 January 1948. Of the 556 members of the Assembly, 207 were Christian Democrats, 115 Socialists and 104 Communists. The government, based on the principle of the coalition of forces that characterised the Resistance, brought together these three fundamental components of national politics. It was led by the head of the DC (Christian Democracy), Alcide De Gasperi, who had been born in the province of Trento in 1881.

De Gasperi was the key figure in the institutional transition from the monarchy to the republic, which, as we have seen, unfolded a few days before the departure of the 'Giro of the Renaissance'. The Republic had won the referendum, but its opponents were trying to gain time through controversial means and delaying tactics. The head of government didn't fall into the trap of those who sought to cause confusion and uncertainty. On 13 June, two days before the departure of the Giro, the last king of Savoy, Humbert II (who had been on the throne since 9 May, following the abdication of his father Victor Emmanuel III), went into exile in Portugal, denouncing the institutional transition as a 'revolutionary' act. De

Gasperi immediately replied that everything had taken place on the basis of the democratic will of the Italian people. And that was that.

The 1946 Giro had four great protagonists; Gino Bartali, who won with an advantage of just 47 seconds; Fausto Coppi, who lost it by only 47 seconds; Giordano Cottur, the rider from Trieste, who won the first stage from Milan to Turin and who was the first to arrive in the city at the end of a dramatic stage; and the crowd, which by its size and enthusiasm was something quite extraordinary. Immense and ever present along roadsides devastated by the war, it was a crowd that seized this sporting opportunity to express the determination and optimism of the new democratic Italy. From the north to the south of the Italian peninsula, the riders were never on their own. From the last bystander to the pope, the Italians were all at their side. In Rome, the riders were received in the Vatican's 'Cortile di San Damaso' by Pius XII who, from the Raphael Rooms, said to them: 'Go, oh brave cyclists of the earthly race and the eternal race!'[33] Cycling to eternity. Sweet music for Gino's ears.

Day after day, little by little, the 1946 Giro (the most important and the most political in the history of the 'Pink Race') unveiled the dimension of the problems facing the Italian people, as well as the hopes of national renaissance that accompanied this sporting competition. Many bridges had been destroyed by bombing or explosives by the retreating Germans, and so riders crossed rivers on boat bridges. During the first stage, from Milan to

Turin, the seventy-nine athletes crossed the Ticino River to Magenta on a temporary wooden bridge. But the more dramatic situation (linked to international tensions and the nascent Cold War) arose from the confusion that reigned over the future of Trieste and the surrounding territory. The new Yugoslavia of Tito, who was already responsible for a bloody 'ethnic cleansing' in the former Italian territories under his control, wanted to occupy Trieste. It relied on well-organized and violent groups of activists, who carried out their activities on the Italian side of the dividing line. The Peace Conference had not yet begun in Paris, and uncertainty about the borders of the new Italy was high. Rome could never imagine giving up Trieste, where power is temporarily exercised by an Allied military administration. Following pressure from Tito, supported at the time by Moscow, this military administration prevented the vote of 2 June 1946 from taking place in the Trieste region. The inclusion of Trieste in the Giro's itinerary was therefore an extremely important political choice. On Sunday, 30 June, the riders pedalled from Rovigo to Trieste when, in the area around Pieris (about 40 kilometres before the finish), they were assaulted by pro-Tito protesters who threw stones at them after leaving nails on the road. Shots were fired and the Italian press denounced the attack on the Giro. On 1 July, *La Gazzetta dello Sport* expressed the national feeling under the headline: 'The race of the people', adding 'in its brilliant day of passion – the extraordinary reception by the Triestines of the Giro d'Italia.'[34] Despite such aggression, the riders decided to go to Trieste, where a crowd awaited them throughout the city and, in particular, at the finish line in the racecourse. The first to cross the line was Giordano Cottur, a living (and pedalling) symbol of Trieste. The other big headline on the front page of *La Gazzetta dello Sport* on 1 July was: '*Promessa mantenuta*' ('Promise kept'). Italy would not give up this city.

The Giro finished a week later at the Milan Arena, where Giordano Cottur was carried aloft in triumph, along with Bartali, the winner of the event. Gino had won his third Giro d'Italia despite not having won a single stage. He had worked to his strengths as only adults know how to do, and was determined, smart and lucky. He wanted this victory and he achieved it. The race (3,000 km – 1,864 miles – in seventeen stages) was very hard: out of the seventy-nine riders at the start, only forty made it to the finish line. The 'Giro of the Renaissance' had given a new youthful boost to Gino the Old, who also won the prize for the best climber.

In 1947, Bartali looked set to win the Milan – San Remo, but after a terrible battle against Coppi in the Dolomites, which the Italian media called the 'Clash of the Titans', he had to settle for second place at the finish line in Milan. This was merely a prologue to a great year of Italian cycling, indeed, cycling and Italy combined. At the beginning of 1948, Bartali had the opportunity, if he so wished, of changing jobs. He could get off his bike and climb into a company car: the DC (Christian

Democracy) wanted him to enter Parliament. National unity shattered in 1947. De Gasperi remained at the head of the government, but, following strong American pressure, socialists and communists were pushed back into opposition. Political controversy raged and a new date, 18 April 1948, was to become decisive for the future of the country as it witnessed the fundamental legislative elections for the democracy of the young country. On one side stood Christian Democracy and on the other, the Popular Front (the Socialist-Communist Coalition). It was a duel without mercy. The Church's support for De Gasperi's party was obvious and continuous, and it was in this context that the Catholic party wanted to enlist Gino as a candidate for the Senate or the Chamber of Deputies. His answer left no room for doubt: he was a sportsman and intended to remain so. He wanted no active part in politics and refused to register with any party. He preferred to pedal rather than speak. Better the cycle than the hemicycle.

De Gasperi triumphed in the legislative elections of 18 April 1948 and although Bartali might not have been a candidate, his images and speeches were still used. The head of the DC now began to form his new government, while the left remained in opposition. Gino's first performances in 1948 gave the Italians the impression that he would have done better to become a senator. The Milan – San Remo was dominated by his dear rival, Fausto Coppi. The headline in *La Gazzetta dello Sport* on 20 March had a certain ecological lyricism: 'Fausto Coppi's latest triumph as he arrives alone at the flowery and luminous finish of San Remo'.[35] During the Giro (won by Fiorenzo Magni), Fausto and Gino engaged in their private battle in the Dolomites. *La Gazzetta's* headline on 5 June read: 'Fausto Coppi's spectacular escape on the snow-covered Falzarego and Pordoi after an emotional duel with Gino Bartali.'[36] Fausto won that stage, but did not go to the Tour de France, which was contested again from 1947. Italian riders, now out of their quarantine, were allowed to compete, but Coppi received a hostile reception. He had already retired from the Giro in protest at the help Magni had received in the Dolomites, and now refused to participate in the Tour as Bartali's 'valet'. Gino fought like a lion to lead the national team there and was successful. Taking the train from Milan to Paris, the old lion was convinced that he had a great opportunity to roar. Perhaps for the last time ...

The 1948 Tour (edition number thirty-five and the second of the post-war period) was particularly tough. Of the 120 riders who started in Paris on 30 June, only 44 arrived in the capital on 25 July. The race was 4,922km (3,058 miles) long over twenty-one stages, including those in the Alps which would take place in difficult weather conditions. At the time, the Tour de France was much longer than it is now in the twenty-first century. In a sign of the times and in a will to build a new Europe, the French race crossed over into Italy, Switzerland and Belgium. The French team was dominated by two characters: Jean Robic, who had won the Tour in 1947, and the great new hope Louison Bobet, who would show his formidable sporting skills during this edition of the race. The 1948 Tour can be considered from two points of view: French and Italian. From the French perspective, it was a very hard and beautiful race, but it was a Tour like many others. For the Italians, it was an event with extraordinary (and beneficial) political and social consequences. In essence it was still a bicycle race, but it can be seen in two different, non-contradictory, ways and the Italian perspective is underlined here: for Italy, this Tour de France was much more of an historic than a sporting event.

For Italy, the turning point in the Tour de France took place on 14 July 1948, a rest day. The cyclists were all resting quietly in their hotels, in homage to the French national holiday, Bastille Day. That same day, Italy was anything but peaceful. The country exploded. In Rome, Palmiro Togliatti, the very skilful and pragmatic secretary general of the PCI (Italian Communist party), was leaving the Montecitorio Palace (seat of the Chamber of Deputies) with his young friend, Senator Nilde Jotti, when a certain Antonio Pallante, a neo-fascist, shot at him three times. Togliatti was seriously injured, but alive. It was 11.30 am and the news shook Italy. Everyone feared the worst. For Togliatti and for the country. A general strike was declared and certain factories were occupied.

Anger turned into protests, which then spilled over and became riots. A civil war was a real possibility. On the left, the revolutionary fanaticists, who had been isolated and neutralised by Togliatti, raised their heads and prepared to remove their weapons from their attics. On the extreme right, the neofascists and monarchists were hoping to take advantage of the chaos. Clashes between protesters and police were bloody: fourteen people were killed on that day alone and a further sixteen in the two days afterwards. In all, around 800 people were injured throughout the country. Firearms were used on both sides. The police were unable to cope and the army was mobilised for mass intervention. The leaders of the PCI were, in turn, very worried about the risks of the demonstrations getting out of hand. They naturally supported the protests, berating the government and the police, but wanted to prevent the protests from becoming a full on insurrection.

For the group of Italians at the Tour, the atmosphere was heavy and tense. On the evening of 14 July, Gino Bartali was in Cannes with the rest of the riders when he received a phone call from a man he knew well. A Catholic who was openly against Mussolini and who was now President of the Council: De Gasperi. Although the actual content of the conversation hovers between reality and legend, it is said that he asked Bartali to do something extraordinary in order to divert the attention of those Italians who were about to cross the red line. Even regardless of the head of government's request,

Bartali understood that his country needed him if they wanted to dream of a peaceful future. The Italians had to think a little more about the Tour and a little less about the revolution. Gino's bike would cross paths with history once again. For the second time in five years, the cycling champion took on a responsibility that was far beyond him. But while in 1943-1944 he had acted in secret, in 1948 Gino was determined to make the front pages of the press so as to attract the Italians' attention and focus their minds on the Tour. Bartali simply *had* to win the Tour de France! He needed to distract his compatriots with an exceptional performance. And he did.

Even those on the left understood the political significance of his sporting endeavour. It was not a question of minimising the gravity of the attack on 14 July, but about wishing to avoid the nascent democracy falling into the trap of a chaos without a future. After successful surgery, Togliatti called for calm. The communist leader – who loved sports and was a supporter of the Juventus football team – was not content to stay abreast of the political situation from his hospital bed. He wanted to know what Bartali's position was in the Tour. It was good: during three consecutive and decisive stages, which would go down in Tour de France history, Gino was carrying out the miracle requested by De Gasperi. It's easy to exaggerate, and even without Gino's Tour victory Italy would have most likely avoided the catastrophe of a widespread revolutionary insurgency. However, the way out of the crisis could indeed have been more difficult and more people could have been injured or killed in the Italian streets. Bartali's exploits in the Tour added to the beneficial effects of Palmiro Togliattii's encouraging medical reports, thereby helping to create a less and less explosive situation throughout the country.

Returning to the actual race, on 14 July the yellow jersey was on the shoulders of Louison Bobet. Bartali was eighth in the general classification, 21 minutes and 28 seconds behind the leader. It was an enormous gap. On the 15th, Gino went on the attack during the mountain stage (which included the Col d'Izoard) from Cannes to Briançon. He won the stage and also climbed up the general classification. He was now in second position and the gap between himself and Bobet was only 1 minute and 6 seconds. *La Gazzetta dello Sport* spoke of 'the spectacular return of Gino and Italian hopes'. On 16 July, in the stage from Briançon to Aix-les-Bains (including the Galibier), Bartali won again and snatched the yellow jersey from Louison Bobet, never relinquishing it until Paris. Following another rest day, the next stage, from Aix-les-Bains to Lausanne, was fought on 18 July. It was Gino the Old's birthday, who celebrated turning 34 with his third consecutive success in the Alps and further strengthened his position in the overall standings. The Tour was now secured. By the time he arrived in Paris on 25 July, his lead was 26 minutes and 16 seconds over

Belgium's Briek Schotte, in second place, and 28 minutes 48 seconds over France's Guy Lapébie, in third. As well as winning the Tour, Gino had also won seven stages and the prize for the best climber. The miracle had become a reality.

Back home, Italians did not yet have television – Rai TV broadcasts would not begin until 1 January 1954 – and so filmed images of the news were available in cinemas, which were often full of people. A *cinegiornale* (newsreel) was available to viewers just before the start of the film. Called *La Settimana Incom*, this weekly newsreel was produced and broadcast from 1946 to 1965. Presenting the images of the Tour's arrival in Paris, *La Settimana Incom* proclaimed: 'Gino, thank you from Italy! Gino, you're great!' The same issue of the newsreel showed images of the priest at Ponte a Ema, don Bartolucci, reading *La Gazzetta dello Sport* as if it were the Gospel. The mixture of sport and religion (very Bartalian) reached its peak with *La Settimana Incom*'s commentary of the Biarritz to Lourdes stage, which Gino had won a week before the attack on Togliatti: 'It's Bartali alone against the whole of France; but the Virgin Mary wants him in first place, on the threshold of her sanctuary!'

When the Tour was finished, the Virgin Mary didn't call Gino, but De Gasperi did. He congratulated him on his victory and thanked him for what he had done for Italy. Bartali replied: 'I only did my duty!' Much later, he would suggest that in the word 'duty' there is indeed a form of citizen responsibility. He would say on TV: 'I only did my job. I behaved like a cyclist. But, if everything had been calm in Italy, I would have fought a battle later. On another stage.'

Even the French were seduced by Gino and gave him a rousing ovation at the end of the Tour. His success was that of Franco-Italian reconciliation. The page of resentment and misunderstandings after the war had been turned. France was at peace with Italy, and Italy was at peace with itself.

One of Paolo Conte's[37] best-known songs is dedicated to this Franco-Italian aspect of Bartali's performance. It alludes to the pre-Tour French mistrust and Gino's challenge to what remained of a somewhat anti-Italian hostility. France was rightly wounded by Mussolini's aggression of 10 June 1940, but, by wanting to participate in the 1948 Tour at all costs and by obtaining such a precious victory, Bartali had shown the existence of an Italy that was truly worthy of respect. For Paolo Conte, the word 'respect' was the real key behind the 1948 transformation. He talks about it in his own way, in the very particular rhythm of his music, emphasising the phrase 'And the French respect us'. He smiles at the French irritation at Gino's success, but believes that this deeply endearing character of the sad, but cheerful, Italian knew how to conquer people's prejudices and banish any bad memories. It was true. In his own way, Bartali had made a significant contribution to the revival of Franco-Italian friendship. Conte's famous song, which you can listen to any time with a simple click on your computer, includes the following lyrics:

Oh, quanta strada nei miei sandali	Oh, how far I got in my sandals
quanta ne avrà fatta Bartali!	How far did Bartali get!
Quel naso triste come una salita	That nose as sad as a steep climb,
quegli occhi allegri da italiano in gita!	Those happy eyes of an Italian on a day trip!
E i francesi ci rispettano	And the French respect us,
che le balle ancora gli girano!	There they are, still pretty annoyed!
Io sto qui e aspetto Bartali	I'll stay here and wait for Bartali
scalpitando sui miei sandali!	Pacing up and down in my sandals!
Da quella curva spunterà	It will come around the bend,
quel naso triste da italiano allegro!	That sad nose of a happy Italian!

11. Gino and Fausto

Three emblematic and highly talked about duos asserted themselves in Italy between the years 1940-1950. These three couples, real or imaginary, both divide and unite the Italian population. They divide it because the characters in question are in an almost perpetual struggle with each other. Since the days of the Guelphs and Gibelins[38] (and even before), the Italians have loved to fight one another. It's a national sport, almost like cycling, which in Bartali's time was more popular than football. But the paradox is that these three pairs of 'dear enemies' sometimes (although not always) managed to agree and unite the people of the charming peninsula which plunges out into the Mediterranean.

The first of these three duos consisted of politicians Alcide De Gasperi and Palmiro Togliatti (Christian Democrat and Communist, respectively), who were both pushing their country forward, even if they could hardly be more different from each other. Trentino De Gasperi, born in Austria in 1881 and elected to the Parliament of Vienna in 1911, spent the most difficult years of fascism behind the walls of the Vatican. His strong values meant he was able to say 'no' to anyone. Even the pope. In 1952, on the eve of the very important election to renew Rome's municipal administration, the possibility of a victory for the social-communist coalition was real. Pope Pius XII was ready to do anything to avoid this happening, including an alliance between Catholics, monarchists and neofascists. The staunch Catholic De Gasperi refused and even though the pope insisted, De Gasperi wouldn't change his mind. Better to lose an election than to lose your soul. The result? He kept his soul and won the election. He had been right, but Pius XII found it difficult to accept and, worse still, he took his revenge. On his thirtieth wedding anniversary, De Gasperi, whose daughter Lucia had just entered the convent, asked the pope for a private audience and a blessing for his family. This time it was the pope's turn to say 'no'.

Born in Genoa in 1893, Palmiro Togliatti spent his years of exile in Moscow where he rubbed shoulders with Stalin, a man with a completely different character: when someone said 'no' to him, he didn't waste time on refusing to give a blessing as his form of revenge, but went straight for the curse – without scrimping on the bullets. Returning to Italy, Togliatti had surprised many people in April 1944 by proposing a very broad agreement to ensure the democratic transition of the country. At the Yalta Conference, Italy was lucky to be located in the West: former exiles in Moscow were well placed to know how lucky he was. They didn't say it openly, of course, but they knew it perfectly well. Alcide and Palmiro argued fiercely in Parliament, but were never disrespectful. On certain points, particularly those which were very sensitive, they even knew how to find common ground. Togliatti often raised his voice against De Gasperi, but gave him the (decisive) votes of Communist MPs when integrating the famous Lateran agreements (which gave Catholicism a very special role in Italy) into the Italian Constitution in 1929. Although maintaining this Mussolinian treaty would have meant avoiding tearing the country apart, it nearly didn't enter the Constitution due to the hostility of the socialists and other secular parties. Consequently, Togliatti summoned the very influential parliamentary journalist Emilio Frattarelli to his office. He asked him to go to De Gasperi and deliver a very confidential message: he [Togliatti] was ready to vote on Article 7 of the future Italian Constitution (the Concordat defined by the Lateran agreements), but wanted to declare so to Parliament before De Gasperi asked him about it publicly. He didn't want to give the impression of having been cajoled into it and so the chief of the DC must let him speak first. Togliatti understood the importance of the Christian religion for Italian workers, but was determined his attitude would not resemble an act of weakness in the face of Vatican pressure. The clever Frattarelli passed the message on to De Gasperi, who in turn agreed to play the game. What's more, in order to keep the Vatican out of the scheme, he informed the pope that the article would probably be rejected. Better to prepare for the worse. Thus, article 7 was approved by both the DC and the PCI. The same idea of the importance of religion to Italian workers would be taken up at the end of 1973 by the communist leader Enrico Berlinguer when launching his project of 'historical compromise' in a series of articles in *Rinascita*, the PCI's intellectual weekly newspaper, founded by Palmiro Togliatti.

The second pair of 'dear enemies' of the new Republican Italy was completely and beautifully imaginary, and almost as caricatural as could be. The whole world knows Don Camillo and Peppone[39]. Time passes, but they are still there. In the context of the Emilian countryside, this delightfully mad couple represents both the Catholics and the Communists (both strictly AOC and 100 per cent organic). Although they quarrelled, they were united when it came to helping the peasants of Brescello, threatened by the flooding of the River Po, or milking the cows who were suffering because of the agricultural workers' strike, determined to assert their rights against landowners who believed that they were allowed to do whatever they wanted.

The third pair in this hopeful and problematic Italy was to be found in the world of sporting rivalry, halfway between ideology and the *commedia dell'arte*. It is, of course, 'our' duo and was comprised of the Catholic Gino Bartali and the transgressive (who was often presented as a pro-communist, even if this was not the case) Fausto Coppi. A symbol of tradition and a symbol of anti-conformism. The 'old' and the 'young', the Tuscan and the Piedmontese. They were sons of the same rural Italy, but Bartali embodied the values of peasant Italy, while Coppi epitomised the spirit of an industrialised country, moving towards new horizons. Bartali was the family man, while Coppi's private life became famous following his relationship with a married woman, Giulia Occhini, known to the whole of Italy as 'The Woman in White'. Bartali was a faithful husband to Adriana. Coppi, although a married man, paid a high price for loving another man's wife. In 1955, Occhini bore him a child, Faustino, after being sentenced to a month's house arrest for 'adultery'. Before the birth, Giulia Occhini left for Buenos Aires; she wanted to give birth in Argentina, where her child could be registered under the name of Coppi. If he had been born in Italy, on the other hand, he wouldn't have been able to bear his father's name as he had been conceived outside of marriage. When speaking of this episode in his book, *Gino Bartali, mio papà*, Andrea Bartali recalls another controversy that took place concerning Coppi's persecution as the result of his relationship with the 'The Woman in White'. In parliament, an MP officially posed the question: 'What is the income of a cyclist if he can afford for his partner to give birth in Argentina?' The result of this questioning was a tax audit of several cycling champions, including Bartali.

As with De Gasperi and Togliatti, and Don Camillo and Peppone, Gino and Fausto sometimes showed unexpected demonstrations of mutual solidarity. One photograph will remain a part of Italian history, proving that rivals can sometimes get along. It is an image as emblematic as it is cryptic. Gino and Fausto are seen passing a water bottle to each other during a mountain stage of the Tour de France in 1952. Although we might not want to know who is passing it to whom, in this instance it is Gino passing it to Fausto, but on other occasions it was the opposite. In times of need, each of the two enemies/friends could help the other, even if, ten minutes later, they would take advantage of their rival's puncture and leave them behind on the Galibier, the Col d'Izoard or the Pordoi Pass. Rivalry: yes. Solidarity: sometimes.

Such emblematic moments of Gino and Fausto's relationship are numerous, starting with the Giro d'Italia of 1940, when they rode together in the *Legnano* team. Coppi was hired to assist the 'number 1' rider, Bartali. But a crash caused by a dog, and other technical incidents prevented Bartali from competing for the pink jersey. Fausto was well placed and the whole team, including Gino, put their money on him. In the Dolomites, the snow, cold and a gastric problem meant that Fausto was in trouble. He was in terrible pain and even wanted to give up while climbing the Pordoi Pass. Gino treated him like you would a child, mixing encouragement with threats. To force him to continue, he reminded him that they both came from peasant families and that their parents had made sacrifices to support their sporting passions. He even went so far as to insult him, accusing him of not having what it took to be a champion. 'Water carrier!' (*Acquaiolo!*), he shouted vehemently. 'You're a water carrier, Coppi! Remember that. Just a water carrier!' There was nothing else to do. Fausto stopped and so

Bartali pushed him into the snow, scooping it up and putting it on his teammate's head and down his beautiful pink jersey. For Fausto, it was like an electric shock and he started pedalling again. At the age of 20, he won his first Giro d'Italia before leaving the *Legnano* to become the 'number 1' rider of the rival team, *Bianchi*. The Gino–Fausto relationship now turned into an open rivalry, often much to the benefit of the sport, but sometimes at the expense of national pride.

The black page of the Gino–Fausto relationship was the world championship in Valkenburg, Holland, on 22 August 1948. Bartali had just won the Tour de France and was in perfect condition. He now wanted the world champion's rainbow jersey. *Bianchi*, Coppi's cycling team, didn't like the idea of a new international triumph for the *Legano* leader. Although they were all united under the national flag, jealousies began to overflow in Valkenburg. This time, the Bartali–Coppi rivalry, further poisoned by *Legnano–Bianchi* hostility, provoked a sporting debacle which caused great harm to the entire country, as well as injuries to the many Italian workers who had arrived from Belgium to follow the race. These Italian miners had been sent to Belgium on the basis of an agreement which the two governments were hesitant to talk about, due to the semi-embarrassing nature of its content. The agreement in question was the 1946 'Migration Protocol' between Italy and Belgium, whereby, in exchange for deliveries of coal at an advantageous price, Italy undertook to send 50,000 workers per year (maximum 35 years of age) to

Belgium. These men would replace the Belgian miners who were reluctant to carry out this hard and dangerous activity. For these men, the trip to Holland was much more than just the fruits of a sporting passion: applauding the victory of Bartali or Coppi meant they could take revenge on fate. However, Bartali and Coppi both lost because they went to war, with one neutralising the other. 'We were mostly afraid of each other; maybe from our shadows as well!'[40], said Gino about this particular moment. The two riders didn't even reach the end of the race and withdrew shortly before the finish line, with the Belgian Alberic Schotte becoming world champion. The Italian migrants had come to watch the race and show the Belgians their national pride, and so the miners whistled profusely at the men who had disappointed them. Over the years, it seems the Italians have forgotten the disappointment of Valkenburg. On the contrary, they should celebrate this sad episode and display the photographs in their living rooms, so as never to forget the risks people take when they tear themselves apart beyond all common sense. Valkenburg's message goes far beyond cycling.

Bartali and Coppi came from two peasant families. Both started working when they were little more than children and lived through the terrible years of the war. Coppi was a prisoner of the English in North Africa from April 1943 to February 1945, when he was brought back to Naples and finally set free. Gino and Fausto entered sporting history, dominating the world of international cycling in the years following the end of the

Second World War. Fausto won the Tour de France in 1949, with Gino finishing second and Jacques Marinelli (French passport but Italian origin) third, and won it again in 1952. Gino won the Giro d'Italia three times (1936, 1937 and 1946) and Fausto five times (1940, 1947, 1949, 1952 and 1953). Fausto finished second in the Giro in 1946 and 1955; Gino in 1947, 1949 and 1950, proving that this duo hold an extraordinary importance in the history of world cycling.

In 1950, the whole of Italy awaited the latest episode of the Gino–Fausto duel and on 4 June, the front cover of the very popular illustrated weekly *La Domenica del Corriere* showed a drawing of the two super-champions in the foreground, with the other race favourites behind them: Bevilacqua, Kubler, Magni and Robic. But on the day the newspaper came out, Coppi had already given up. On 2 June, during the stage from Vicenza to Bolzano (the last stage of the Giro Bartali won), Fausto crashed and was seriously injured. On arriving in Rome (a very rare occasion as the race usually ends in Milan), Gino was second in the overall rankings behind the Swiss Hugo Koblet, the first foreigner to win the Giro d'Italia. He aimed to take revenge during the Tour de France, in which Fausto was obviously unable to participate.

As far as Bartali was concerned, the story of the 1950 Tour de France turned out to be very difficult. Still thinking of his own problems, he sent a very harsh message to the *tifosi* (supporters) in general and to French *tifosi* in particular. It was a message against violence. This time, however, he did it without Coppi, who didn't take part in the Tour that year. Out on the roads, Gino was the victim of what he considered to be a genuine attack on the part of the French *tifosi*. He wanted to express his indignation loudly and clearly, and he did so in his own way. Through anger. Of course, violent, intolerant and unsportsmanlike people exist everywhere, in France as well as in Italy. And, of course, they are only a small minority of this enthusiastic and extraordinary crowd which, in most cases, admires and applauds the riders. But during the 1950 Tour de France, certain enthusiasts attacked the Italian cyclists, especially Bartali, with particular aggressiveness. After winning the Tour in 1948 and 1949, the Italians were also in a very good position in the 1950 edition, which could have seen the first victory of Fiorenzo Magni. On 25 July 1950, the riders were in the Pyrenees and the stage from Pau to Saint-Gaudens was won by Gino. At the same time, Fiorenzo Magni took the yellow jersey. On 26 July the Tour climbed the Col d'Aspin. Here, groups of enthusiasts attacked Gino, who they believed was responsible for bringing down the Frenchman Jean Robic. They tried to destabilise him and make him crash, provoking him, shaking him up and throwing things at him. Despite the correct response of the organisers towards what had happened, Gino believed that the Tour should be abandoned. He put his prestige and popularity on the line by persuading all the Italian riders to leave the Tour at the end of the twelfth stage (Saint-Gaudens to Perpignan), on 26 July 1950.

Consequently, Fiorenzo Magni missed the opportunity of a lifetime to win the Tour de France.

The Tour was finally won by Fredi Kübler, the first Swiss to triumph at the race. Fortunately, in the midst of so many images showing Gino on edge, a photograph full of optimism would enter the wonderful history of the Tour de France. It shows the handshake between Gino and the great American actor Orson Welles, who gave the signal for the start of the race in central Paris, between the Royal Palace and the Louvre, on 13 July 1950. Orson Welles is smiling and shaking hands with Gino, who is seen wearing a jersey in the Italian colours (at this time the Tour was organised around national teams), with the name of his particular team, created by himself and which bore his name, sewn on.

The unpleasant experiences of the summer of 1950 didn't sit well in Italian sport, and cycling historians will always wonder why Gino was so adamant in his determination to demand the withdrawal of the Italians. Of all the Italians.

Gino the Old certainly felt the burden at a very particular moment in autumn 1953. On Sunday, 18 October he was travelling to Switzerland by car with friends to take part in a race in Lugano, when their car was violently hit by another vehicle in Lombardy. The next day, the Italian press published a photograph of a seriously injured Gino in his hospital bed. Two news items dominated the front page of the Roman daily *Il Messaggero*: the inability of the international community to decide on the future of Trieste; and 'Gino Bartali injured in a serious car accident'. Coppi went to visit him in hospital and they joked about the past and the future. In 1954 Gino was back on his bike, but it was obvious that he couldn't continue. He participated in forty races and won once. It was to be his last. He officially announced his retirement on 9 February 1955, at the age of 40. Fausto, however, would never officially announce his retirement.

The very complicated relationship between Gino and Fausto included two parallel family tragedies. As we have already seen, in June 1936 Gino lost his younger brother Giulio, who was also a cyclist, in a road accident during a race. Serse Coppi, Fausto's younger brother and the loyalest among the other riders in his team (*Bianchi*), also died in June 1951 following a crash during the Giro del Piemonte. Although it only appeared trivial at first, the accident turned out to be lethal. During the final sprint of the race, on the outskirts of Turin, the wheel of his bike caught in the tramlines causing him to fall and hit his head violently against the ground. He was, however, able to stand up and re-mount his bicycle. There didn't appear to be any serious damage done and at the finish line he spoke to Bartali, who found him 'much more talkative, open and extroverted than his brother Fausto'. Later on, however, he lost consciousness and died. He was 28. Giulio Bartali had died at 19. Just as Gino had done in 1936 the day after Giulio's death, in 1951 Fausto Coppi also intended to abandon the sport following the death of his brother. The two champions bore an unbearable feeling of guilt for the death of their respective younger brothers, who had loved and appreciated them so much, and who had dreamed of imitating or simply helping them by pedalling alongside them.

The difference between Gino and Fausto came from their sporting rivalry, but also their characters. Curzio Malaparte wrote: 'If Bartali radiated human warmth, Coppi radiated a feeling of profound loneliness'. (*The Two Faces of Italy: Coppi and Bartali*, Pasciutto, 2007). Gino summed up the situation by saying:

> *There was always the following difference between myself and Coppi: I had a closed and wild character, but I always stayed strong and my morale never dropped below the safeguard. On the other hand, Fausto, although endowed with all the characteristics of a great champion, let himself go a little; a few seconds lost in a race was enough to shatter and destroy his morale.*

Bartali talks about his own character using the expression 'closed and wild', while he defines that of Fausto Coppi as 'closed and shy'. The two therefore have two opposite ways of being 'closed', that is to say, focussed on their job. Gino was 'wild', an explosive closed, an embodiment of the 'open closed' tautology. Whereas Fausto tended to shut himself up as if to protect himself from the outside world. Gino spoke very readily, sometimes too willingly, while Fausto was embarrassed in front of the microphones.

Their *tifosi* loved them just as they were, with a genuine passion. Italy in the 1950s was divided into two factions: Gino's *tifosi* and Fausto's, the '*bartaliani*' and the '*coppiani*'. You couldn't be Italian without joining one or other of these 'parishes'. The idea of the 'traditional' Bartali and 'transgressive' Coppi became stereotypes. A simple memory might be enough to find oneself 'lost' in one group or the other, that of the *coppiani* or the *bartaliani*. Maria found love on the day of Ginettaccio's victory at the end of Pau – Lourdes; Marco caught his ferry in the morning when Coppi (nicknamed *l'airone*, the heron) was in solitary flight on the Galibier. The important thing was loyalty. Once your were *bartaliani* or *coppiani*, you remained so. They were militant, quarrelling with members of the rival party. Families were torn apart, even during Christmas dinner. Celebrities were quick to show their affinities. Sports journalist Gianni Brera was a *coppiano*. One of the Communist leaders, Giancarlo Pajetta, was a *bartaliano*, as was Domenico Modugno, the composer of the song *Volare*.

The passion of the *bartaliani* and *coppiani* also found its way into the magic of the small screen. In 1959, the national broadcaster, Rai, had only one television channel and its programmes were immensely popular. In the midst of an 'economic miracle', the Italian population would meet on Saturday evenings in bars and at friends' apartments equipped with a television in order to watch the programme *Il Musichiere*, hosted by the very famous (and much-loved) presenter, Mario Riva. The show would begin with the smooth notes of the song *Domenica è sempre domenica* ('Sunday is always Sunday'). Bartali and Coppi were both guests and played on their popularity as brother-enemies by showing off in front of an audience who loved seeing them together. The Italian people were greedy for nostalgia, so often served up by the 'wonderful' technology of television. At that time, Bartali and Coppi were shooting commercials together for Arrigoni stock cubes. The cliché of dispute and reconciliation was always the same. They would tear each other apart when talking about the old races when Bartali, while tasting the broth, would declare that he found it delicious and to which Coppi would reply: 'If you like it, then it must be disgusting!' By the end they would obviously agree on the quality of the broth and the slogan declared: 'Broth for champions with Arrigoni cubes!'[41] First class broth and likewise memories.

In Mario Riva's *Il Musichiere*, our heroes did much more than just warm up the old broth of their proverbial rivalry and their newfound peace. They answered the question: 'Who is the greatest cycling champion?' Bartali went first. 'It's Coppi', he said, while the latter, of course, said that it was Bartali. When watched today (which you can do thanks to the internet), the show inspires tenderness and emotion and seems wonderfully naive. The Iron Man and the Heron talked and sang, giving the impression of acting out a well prepared role, while their somewhat theatrical embarrassment reveals a simplicity of being men of the people. The two men, aged 45 and 40, are completely authentic, with no need to put on an act.

An unforgettable moment, the climax of the 1959 show, came when they started a duet of the famous (Italian) song *Come pioveva!* (It was Raining so Hard!), based on alleged polemics of their old rivalry. Bartali sang 'on the snow-capped Alps the challenges we faced'. And Coppi replied: 'Yes, but it's you who lost!' The Italians sat in front of their television sets were thrilled. It was as if they could almost touch their idols: 'What a wonder this magic black and white box is! It's going to change the world, believe me!' 'You are right, my dear Mr. Rossi! I'm going to take out a loan to buy one; then I'll take out another one for the *Seicento!*'

While appearing on *Il Musichiere*, the two champions spoke about the Tour de France and the times when they had helped each other out. Bartali sang: 'Do you remember the day I waited for you in Saint-Malo?' This refers to an incident in July 1949, shortly after the Valkenburg controversy, when the Italian team (with ex-racer Alfredo Binda as the technical director), took part in the Tour de France. Gino and Fausto had promised to help each other and on 4 July, during the fifth stage (Rouen to Saint-Malo), Coppi was the victim of a crash. Demoralised, he wanted to give up, but Bartali and the others waited for him and helped him stay in the race, even if it meant he was now almost 37 minutes behind the leader, Jacques Marinelli, in the general classification. He began to climb up the rankings during the time trial stage and continued to do so in the Pyrenees. In the Alps, Gino and Fausto were in eighth and ninth positions respectively, while the yellow jersey was now on the shoulders of their teammate, Fiorenzo Magni. The Tour continued in difficult stages, from Cannes to Briançon, and from Briançon to Aosta. On 18 July Gino and Fausto both dominated the first of these stages, with only a void behind them, or almost. Gino punctured during the descent towards Briançon, but Fausto waited to help him and Gino went on to win the stage and take the yellow jersey from Magni. It was a great way to celebrate his thirty-fifth birthday. On 19 July the stage finished in Italy and all of the Italian journalists discussed the chivalrous behaviour of the two champions. As on the previous day, the two were involved in a breakaway on the Petit-Saint-Bernard. Once more Gino punctured during the descent and Fausto waited for him. Valkenburg was now certainly nothing more than a bad memory. Unfortunately for Gino, the era of recriminations was not quite over as he crashed shortly after the puncture. Coppi was waiting again for him when a biker from the RAI radio network, sent by the Italian team director Alfredo Binda, pulled up to tell him to forget his colleague and set off alone for the stage victory and the yellow jersey. He did as he was told and took Bartali's jersey, which he would keep until Paris. Gino felt betrayed, but by Binda, not by Fausto.

Recalling this story ten years later as a joke during a TV show was a way for everyone (Gino and Fausto as well as the *bartaliani* and *coppiani*) of closing the book on old quarrels. It was much more than a show. It was about resilience, and it wasn't over yet. Still singing, Gino and Fausto tackled another very controversial episode, when Coppi reminded Bartali that he once 'pushed him on the Col d'Aspen'. Immediately afterwards he called him 'my commander', as he had done in 1940, at the start of his professional racing career, before he left to join the *Bianchi* team and he was at Gino's 'service' in the *Legnano* team.

With scripts carefully prepared by the channel's writers, the musical duo ended with lyrics sung in unison. As one man, Gino and Fausto sang:

We were rivals, but friendly
We were enemies, but always loyal
The hostility that divided us
What was it like! What was it like!

The *come pioveva!* of the famous song became 'What was it like!' The friction between Gino and Fausto (often loyal and sometimes less so) pleased the Italians enormously. They entertained them, represented them, reassured them, and brought them together, a little like Alcide and Palmiro and Don Camillo and Peppone. Thank you both.

12. 'I'm always chasing something!'

At the time of the *Il Musichiere* show in 1959, Gino Bartali and Fausto Coppi were genuine friends with lots of projects in common, including a sports team, commenting on races for the media, taking part in television shows and a little advertising for various different products. Gino was full of ideas which he would promote with Fausto and there were certainly enough to raise a glass (sparkling, thanks to the bubbles of its content: San Pellegrino mineral water). They were a dynamite team. Bartali, now a sports manager, and Coppi, still on his bike. Together again as they were in 1940. United by the desire to find a new Gino and Fausto among the young European riders, the new *San Pellegrino* cycling team aimed to be a breeding ground for talent. From now on, Bartali and Coppi's team would be a place for dreams and new ideas. Cheers!

On 10 December 1959, Fausto left for a working holiday in Africa for a few days. As well as taking part in sporting exhibitions in Ouagadougou, in what at the time was called Upper Volta (the future Burkina Faso), a group of cycling champions (including Jacques Anquetil and Raphaël Géminiani) also had the opportunity to go on a safari. Coppi loved hunting and was passionate about this trip. Gino was his friend, as well as his sporting director, and when Fausto told him about the trip and asked for his consent to go, Gino didn't disappoint him. Coppi was happy and set off for the last adventure of his career. And of his life. Once back in their homeland, Géminiani and Coppi began to suffer increasing discomforts, including tremors and very high fevers. After the failure of the initial treatments, Géminiani was seen by a specialist in tropical medicine (or 'colonial medicine' as it was known in France at the time), who, following blood analysis carried out by the Pasteur Institute, finally knew what the problem was. The French cyclist had caught malaria and his days were numbered unless he swallowed massive doses of quinine immediately. In Italy, Coppi was suffering the exact same symptoms as Géminiani and so the latter's family contacted the Italian cyclist's doctors. Sadly, they ignored the information and persisted in their misdiagnosis, and consequently their treatment. This was quite strange as Italians know malaria very well, the plague having long raged in the country, where swampy areas (the natural home of mosquitoes) were numerous; from north to south and passing through the Tuscan Maremma. Italians knew malaria so well that from the end of the nineteenth century, quinine was produced directly by the state and sold at low prices not only in pharmacies, but in tobacco shops. But Coppi's doctors weren't thinking about malaria and quinine. And so the two victims of the same condition received completely different treatments. Géminiani survived, but Coppi died on 2 January 1960 at the hospital in Tortona, Piedmonte.

He was both a victim of malaria and his doctors, a very dangerous cocktail of incompetence and presumption.

Fausto's death left Gino without his former rival who had since become a true friend. They had become almost each other's brothers, but now one of them was gone. For Gino, it was an opportunity to revisit his past and perhaps even be tempted to talk about something other than sport. Had the time now come to tell the general public about his experiences during the war? The answer was no and he chose to continue as before, with his faith, his family and his secret, which he would hold on to for another twenty years, until another person entered the scene and information began to circulate in several countries about the 'network of two religions'.

In 1978 there began to be talk in the United States about the rescue of Italian Jews during the war. In New York, *The Assisi Underground: The Priests Who Rescued Jews* was published by the writer and director Alexander Ramati, whose real name was David Solomonovich Grinberg. The author chose to highlight the work of Father Rufino Niccacci, who claimed to have known Bartali during the war when he was the father guardian of the San Damiano Monastery in Assisi. Niccacci and Ramati had first met in 1944 following the liberation of Umbria, before meeting again in Israel in 1974, where the former was coming from Assisi on a pilgrimage to the Holy Sepulcher, and the latter from Hollywood for a conference at the university. Their friendship that had begun in Assisi resumed once more in Jerusalem. Rufino

Niccacci died in 1976, two years before the release of Ramati's book, in which he was the protagonist. The work, translated into Italian three years later, offered Gino a new opportunity to talk about a story where he too played a role. His actions in Assisi as a courier carrying false documents was among Father Rufino's memories, as well as those of the Clare sisters at the Saint-Quirico convent. It wasn't a question of seeking personal glory, but simply of making a contribution to the reconstruction of the history of this troubled period. But nothing was to be said.

As far as Gino's story was concerned, however, there were two exceptions to this: his family and Rabbi Nathan Cassuto. In the first case, there was the testimony of his son, Andrea, while in the second there was the story (repeated much later by Yad Vashem) of Sara Corcos Di Gioacchino, sister of Anna Cassuto Di Gioacchino. Anna had been arrested in Florence in December 1943 and deported in January 1944, along with her husband Nathan Cassuto. Documents presented to Yad Vashem in the twenty-first century show that Bartali initially refused Sara Corcos' request for a meeting regarding his actions during the war. However, after mentioning that she was a member of Nathan Cassuto's family, emotions were clearly stirred in Gino and he agreed to speak privately, but without anything being recorded. Bartali had obviously always had a great respect and admiration for Rabbi Nathan Cassuto, a key figure in the 'network of two religions'.

Consequently, apart from these exceptional situations, Gino was always faithful to his own rules of maintaining silence. After the release of the Italian edition of Ramati's book in 1981, Gino believed that any testimony from him might be considered as showing off. He spoke a great deal on a variety of subjects, but continued to remain silent about the help he gave to the persecuted. It was Ramati, therefore, who helped spread the word about a very significant chapter in the Second World War, such was the merit of his work.

Alexander Ramati, a Polish Jew, was born in 1921 in Brest-Litovsk, in the territory of present-day Belarus. On 17 June 1944, the day Assisi was liberated, he was part of General Montgomery's British 8th Army as they entered Assisi: the town of Saint Francis, of Bishop Nicolini, his right hand man Father Brunacci and the dynamic Brother Niccacci. The young Polish soldier read a banner expressing the desire to bury all racism for good. For a Polish Jew like him, this was wonderful to see. Ramati wanted to know the protagonists of the clandestine network which had saved the lives of over 300 Jews (mainly, but not only, Italian) in Assisi alone by hiding them in monasteries. In June 1944 Ramati discovered the determination that had been shown by the bishop and his collaborators, as well as the courage of the printers, Luigi and Trento Brizi (who made the false identity papers), of Giuseppina Biviglia, Abbess of the Clarisse di San Quirico Convent, and Ermella Brandi, Mother Superior of the Stigmatine Sisters Convent.

In the twenty-first century these names (the five monks and nuns and the two printers) were added to the list of the 'Righteous' in the Yad Vashem Memorial, along with that of Gino Bartali.

In Assisi in 1944, Ramati discovered the extraordinary story of how a small town of 4,500 inhabitants sheltered 4,000 refugees, including hundreds of Jews who had been victims of racial discrimination. The miracle of Assisi was the result of the special atmosphere created in the shadow of St Francis' Basilica. 'During this period of the war, Assisi was in a very particular situation, characterised by the will and the courage of several characters, despite being on opposite sides, including the chief of the German military forces, Colonel Valentin Müller, and the fascist *podestà* (mayor) Arnaldo Fortini', says journalist Marina Rosati, who created the Museum of Memory in this Umbrian city. Müller, the commander of the German troops occupying the city, was a Bavarian doctor. A devout Catholic, he attended Mass every morning in St Francis' Basilica and maintained a cordial relationship with Bishop Nicolini, the brains behind the plan to rescue the Jews. Müller could well have known much more than he let on, but he did his best not to know too much, preferring to turn a blind eye. It is even said that he directly rescued certain people whom other Germans wanted to deport or execute. Müller was mainly responsible for organising a Wehrmacht medical network in Assisi, located in religious institutions that were made available by the bishop. There were dozens of convents and monasteries in the town, and while some were used to house the administrations, others were used to treat wounded German soldiers. The whole city became both a large hospital and a centre for helping all kinds of refugees. The Americans were aware of the situation and, in the absence of fundamental strategic objectives, they carefully avoided any bombing and air strikes. In August 1944, after the terrible battle of Monte Cassino, the Germans were forced to leave Assisi before the Allies advanced further. Colonel Müller was determined to avoid the retreating German soldiers from taking revenge against the civilian population, as well as the immense artistic heritage of the city, which includes, among other things, the famous frescoes by Giotto in St Francis' Basillica. The head of the German forces personally kept an eye on sensitive locations to prevent acts of hatred and vandalism. The city of Assisi, where Gino Bartali had visited several times, was therefore a microcosm of common sense in the midst of a violent world. A flag for the 'power of good', which brings to mind the book by Marek Halter, published by Robert Laffont in 1995 and bearing the same title. As the author says, everyone must know that 'in times dominated by cowards and killers, there were individuals who allowed us not to despair of the humanity of men and women who didn't hesitate to risk death to save lives'.

In the early 1980s, America was sensitive to *The Assisi Underground: The Priests Who Rescued Jews* and the story of the people of Umbria and Tuscany reached the White House. On 11 April 1983, the President of the

United States, Ronald Reagan, was speaking to Jews who had survived Nazi persecution, and said: 'The picturesque town of Assisi, Italy, sheltered and protected 300 Jews. Father Rufino Niccacci organised the effort, hiding people in his monastery and in the homes of parishioners.' Assisi thus obtained an additional consecration, and was recognised more than ever as a global emblem of courage and good will.

Next was the step from book to film, which Ramati took in 1984. *Assisi Underground* was released the following year and broadcast to the Italian public by Rai. The character of Gino Bartali is seen arriving by bike at a monastery in Assisi, bringing the necessary photographs for the false identity papers, which he would then smuggle to Florence himself, hiding them in his bicycle. Italians soon began to understand the importance of the secret Jewish aid networks during the Second World War, and Bartali could no longer pretend that nothing had happened. However, he reacted by staying true to his good old grumpy character. How could people talk about him without having consulted him? It was unbelievable! He was angry, just like the stereotypical '*Tuscanaccio*', the Tuscan male who didn't care for diplomacy or half measures. It is often said that in Tuscany, people start with insults and only afterwards turn to dialogue. Gino issued threats: he wanted to be the only one who could talk about his past. But he had no desire to do so and therefore continued not to. However, he finally realised that there was nothing wrong with Alexander Ramati's work, as a novel and as a testimony and investigation. There were inaccuracies and even errors, but the story was what counted, and the bottom line was that Ramati paid tribute to a town and to a people who deserved it. Resigned to others talking about his story, Bartali preferred not to participate in the avalanche of revelations that followed the screening of the film. The 'Lion of Tuscany', as Gino was also nicknamed by the Italian press, continued to be involved in cycling and to appear on light entertainment shows.

For example, he appeared on a Rai television programme alongside Vittorio Gassman. The programme, *Il Mattatore* (The Matador), was also the Italian title of a film in which Gassman had starred. Bartali talked about cycling races and intervened several times on a variety of subjects, endlessly repeating his famous phrase known by all Italians: '*È tutto sbagliato, è tutto da rifare!*', ('It's all wrong, do it all again!'). It's a sentence that reveals his character as a dissident, always ready to question things in the name of his insatiable thirst for justice. Every evening from 13 January to 18 April 1992, Bartali took part in the satirical programme *Striscia la Notizia*; a parody of the daily news and broadcast by the private channel Canale 5. The show was the product of the imagination of an Italian TV executive who, by chance, had the same name (Antonio Ricci) as the imaginary protagonist of the film *The Bicycle Thief*, quoted in the first chapter of this book. In his new role as a 'journalist' for a fake satirical news programme, the real Gino never stopped saying his favourite phrase, according to which it is absolutely necessary to 'do it all again!'. Prophetic words.

As Bartali repeated his famous saying on television, magistrates in Milan were actually starting to make history with the investigation that would go down with the infamous name, *Mani pulite* (Clean Hands). On Monday, 17 February 1992, a member of the Socialist Party (Mario Chiesa, director of the hospice for the elderly in Milan) was arrested by the carabinieri just after receiving a bribe. Italian politics was shook to its foundations. Other revelations would follow and so (even after Bartali's death) his message of 'it's all wrong, do it all again!' would (unfortunately) remain relevant for Italians. But Bartali's legacy certainly doesn't come down to just one controversial phrase. His true legacy is his message of having love and determination for one's work, and is expressed by these words from the writer Dino Buzzati: 'Bartali was the living symbol of human endeavour'. (*Bartali è stato il vivo simbolo del lavoro umano*).

Gino died of a heart attack at his home in Florence on 5 May 2000. He had spent his last years surrounded by his family, his wife Adriana, and their three children Andrea, Luigi and Bianca Maria, with whom he was very close. He continued to envisage new ideas and projects until his final days, saying: 'I'm always chasing something!'[42] It was as if, even in the warmth of his family environment, life was always an eternal chase for him, but as of 5 May 2000, it was now the others who must chase him.

New research and revelations meant that in April 2006, the Italian Republic, represented by President Carlo Azeglio Ciampi, awarded Gino Bartali the Gold Medal for Civil Valour, which was presented to his wife, Adriana. In turn, experts from the Yad Vashem Memorial decided in 2013 to officially recognise Gino Bartali's role during the war, a choice which fitted perfectly into the logic of the Jerusalem Memorial. As Gabriele Nissim notes in his book *Le Jardin des Justes* (The Garden of the Righteous), Moshe Bejski, the long-running president of Yad Vashem's Righteous Among the Nations Commission, had been seeking 'people around the world who had risked their lives to help the Jews during Nazi persecution'. According to Nissim, Bejski 'was not interested in the purity and perfection of human beings, he was not looking for heroes or supermen', but he wanted 'to remember those who, in the face of extreme evil legitimised by law, had tried to save even one life from those who had simply behaved like men'. This was his definition of the Righteous. Among those who testified to Yad Vashem about Bartali's actions in 1943-1944 was Giorgio Goldenberg, whose photograph Bartali dedicated to him in 1941 is now in the Memorial's archives. He had been forced to change his name to Giorgio Goldini to make it more 'Italian', but in Israel he was called Shlomo Goldenberg-Paz, an even more Jewish name than his original one. The documentation on Bartali at Yad Vashem includes the rescue of Jews hidden at his home in Florence (the Goldenbergs and, for a shorter period, their cousin Aurelio Klein, who then left for Switzerland thanks to false papers), aid to Jewish families in Tuscany (including the testimony of Giulia Donati Baquis, who was in Lido di Camaiore, where Bartali delivered false identity papers) and Gino's work as a 'courier of freedom' between Florence and Assisi. Renzo Ventura explained to historians at Yad Vashem that his mother, Marcella Frankenthal-Ventura, had told him that Bartali had delivered false papers for herself, her parents and her sister on behalf of Elia Dalla Costa's (the Archbishop of Florence) network. Yad Vashem's conclusion was clear: 'Bartali, a courier of the Resistance, played an important role in the rescue of Jews as part of the network created by Rabbi Nathan Cassuto, in which Dalla Costa was also involved'.

Andrea Bartali, Gino's eldest son, died in 2017. He had been involved in the study and promotion of his father's sporting life and work during the Second World War for a long time. To highlight Gino's link with Assisi and with the clandestine network behind the false documents, Andrea's daughters, Gioia and Stella, offered the small private chapel in their grandfather's Florentine home to the town's Museum of Memory in 2018. When asked about his father's silence on his humanitarian activities in 1943-1944, Andrea replied with a quote that his father had entrusted to him:

> *I want to be remembered for my sporting achievements and not as a war hero. The heroes are the others, those who suffered in body, mind, and in their loved ones.*

*I just did what I did best. Ride a bike. Good must be
done discretely. Once it is spoken of it loses its value
because it is as if one is trying to draw attention away
from the suffering of others. They are the medals you
can hang on your soul that will count in the Kingdom
of Heaven, not on this earth.*[43]

These words perfectly encompass Gino Bartali. The
cheeky, rather wild character, the extreme generosity,
the solidarity with the misfortunes of others and a faith
in fundamental values. His was an authentic and sincere
faith. A faith that might not have moved mountains, but
certainly helped to climb them.

Afterword

Among the great many joys of my job I had the pleasure of having known Gino Bartali and being able to speak with him at length. The first time, intimidated, I pissed him off. He, meanwhile, was abrupt: don't forget that in cycling we're not as formal! He's the one who broke the ice, to hell with our thirty-one year age difference. Gino had already stopped racing, but he was still at the Giro: either as a columnist for *La Gazetta dello Sport*, with always-tasty articles, or as an ambassador, perhaps today one could even say he was representing a commercial brand. He drove an open-top car for Vittadello clothes or Giordani bikes, always wearing a cycling cap and driving with one hand, the other hand greeting fans while holding the inevitable cigarette.

What joy, as I said. As a journalist and human being. Journalist because several times, including when discussing the stage from Cannes to Briançon following the 1948 attack on the communist leader Togliatti, I gathered my reports on the event from Gino himself. He was an honest man, even in the small things. He wasn't a fake. When I started on this voyage of discovery I felt like a child. The 1938 Tour de France? My parents didn't even meet until two years later. The child was waiting for his uncle to tell him stories. True stories, not fairy tales, of a world that already fascinated him for its humanity and for the number of adventures he could embark on. Gino both impressed and frightened others because of his hoarse voice, typical of the regular smoker. The problem was also the result of a bizarre bet he'd made when he was a child, aged 7, in Tuscany, when he was buried in the snow by his playmates saying it was only 'for a few hours'. When he was little he looked fragile and was called Careggi, after a hospital in Florence. When he became an adult, however, he was known as the Iron Man. Another great Italian cyclist, Alfredo Martini, who was also from Tuscany, once told me that Bartali was never too cold or too hot. For Gino, extreme weather conditions were almost a joy.

That day in July 1948, when he took part in the unforgettable stage from Cannes to Briançon, the departure was at 6 am. He woke up around 4 for breakfast, a quick massage, and a meeting with the other members of his team. It was raining. Bartali lit his usual cigarette, without a filter, and went to see Louison Bobet, the wearer of the yellow jersey. He said to him: 'Today, one of us isn't going to have fun'. Bobet already had the look of one who was going to lose. He was more than 21 minutes ahead of Gino, and would end up losing 20 minutes by the end of the day. His defeat would be complete by the next satge. Bartali told me that on 14 July 1948 he spent time on the beach in Cannes with his friends to celebrate his birthday. They were drinking vermouth and eating a fruit pie when the hotel owner arrived on the beach saying, 'Mister Bartali, there's a telephone call from Italy'. At the other end of the line was one of Gino's acquaintances, Bartolo Paschetta, vice-president of Catholic Action, who passed him on to Prime Minister De Gasperi. 'Gino, could you win the Tour?' 'I don't know, your excellencey. But I'll probably win tomorrow's stage from Cannes to Briançon.' 'Well done,' said De Gasperi, 'please, we need good news here in Italy.'

At the time, there was talk among the Italian team's entourage in Cannes about the attack against the secretary general of the Communist Party. Italian journalists were organising their luggage to return home and went to greet Bartali at the end of 14 July, which was a rest day for the Tour de France. The riders were hearing very alarming reports from Italy. There had been a revolt, shots were fired, thirty people were dead, it was revolution, civil war. Gino tried, unsuccessfully, to speak to his wife in Florence. Dinner at the hotel seemed more like a funeral vigil. Nobody wanted to speak as concern and anxiety filled the air. Bartali didn't give up a his few glasses of red wine or his cigarettes. His doctor had suggested that he smoke occasionally in order to stimulate his heart, which beat at an incredibly slow rate, and Gino had since found a taste for cigarettes. On the evening of 14 July 1948, he wanted to talk to the other Italian cyclists. He said very few words: 'Guys, tomorrow may be our last day at the Tour de France. We may be forced to go home. So tomorrow we must achieve something extraordinary.'

Gino told me all about what had happened, in the open top car during a stage of the Giro d'Italia, and at the time I could clearly see his enormous popularity throughout the whole country. Genuine popularity, not just people hunting autographs. Everyone dreamed of receiving their photograph. Bartali always had some colour ones with him, pre-signed, and each time the car stopped someone spoke to him saying that he'd seen him race one day, or had given him a water bottle on the legendary stages of the Passo della Scoffera or the climb at Macerone. Another told him that he knew his mechanic, while someone else said that he'd completed his military service in Gino's home city of Florence. Everyone had something to say to him. We had our photograph taken together and then went to the bistro to drink red wine. The crowd around Bartali's car gave me the impression of a secular procession, with the former champion in place of the patron saint. However, I never told Gino about this feeling as I was afraid of hurting his Catholic sensibility. I can still remember the voice of the crowd as his car arrived during a stage of the Giro d'Italia: 'C'è Gino, sta arrivando Gino!' ('Gino's here, Gino's coming!') People were clapping, women were blowing kisses. One day, during a stage of the Tour de France in the 1930s, he refused to be photographed alone with Josephine Baker, saying: 'I'm engaged'.

When we were together to follow the Giro d'Italia, he said to me: 'You see, I won a lot of money during my career, but we must never forget that our last shroud will have no pockets. My real wealth is made up of those hands that pressed mine, the glass of red wine I was offered, and the place at the table so many Italian families offered me.' When he returned home at the end of the legendary 1948 Tour, he had little thought for money. De Gasperi invited him to Rome to thank him for his achievements and said, 'You gave us a huge gift and you deserve one as well. What do you want?' Bartali's response: 'Excellency, I'd like to spend a year without paying taxes.' Giulio Andreotti, De Gasperi's young right-hand man, intervened by saying: 'No, that's impossible' and so Bartali decided: 'In that case, I don't want anything at all.'

Even when he was old, Bartali remained the Iron Man. I remember an evening at the Osteria del Treno restaurant, Milan, in 1993. I'd edited an anthology of texts from the famous Italian journalist Gianni Brera, who had recently died, and had invited his sporting friends and writers to present the book. Among the former athletes was Gino, 79 years old at the time. Seated at his table were Mario Fossati, one of the best cycling writers, along with Ottavio Missoni and his wife Rosita, and Fabio Capello and his wife Laura. They were all sports-related characters and got along famously. Bartali spoke almost continuously, but not because of his desire to be the star of the evening, rather because the others kept asking him questions. Knowing he was not a night owl, I'd asked my friend Carlo Pierelli, who had driven cars during countless tours of Italy and France, to bring him back to the hotel at around 1 am. It was no use. 'Guys, if we can't find cards to play then I'll go to sleep,' said Gino at 3:55 am. We all went to sleep, exhausted. He was as fresh as a daisy.

Fascism defined Jews as 'enemies of the state', and those who aided them during the Italian Social Republic risked imprisonment, deportation and even their lives. For 800 of them, as well as other anti-fascists, Bartali was their saviour. Life had given him joys and pains too: a younger brother who'd died from an accident in a cycling race, and a son who'd been born dead during the war in Florence due to the curfew, as no doctors were ready to take the risk of driving at night. Bartali was a cultural anti-fascist: a concrete, peasant culture that didn't come from books. He'd only studied until primary school before leaving to start work, and his 'university' had been the streets of Florence. His Catholicism was deeply rooted in him and suggested he draw a line between good and evil. The fascist regime was aware of all this, and the Ministry of Popular Culture had consequently made specific arrangements: newspapers should only deal with him in the event of a major sporting victory, without ever amplifying their articles with praise.

In 1938 the Italian football team won its second world title on French soil by playing in black jerseys (the colour of fascism) and making the fascist salute in front of the crowd. In return, the crowd, full of French and Italian exiles, whistled and booed at the gesture. Back in Rome, the national football team was received with great pomp by Mussolini at Palazzo Venezia.

Shortly after, Bartali won the Tour de France, but no one invited him to il Duce's residence. Being an honest man, Gino couldn't stand arrogance and as a result there was an incompatibility between himself and fascism. The fascists wanted to impose their sporting calendar on him: 'No Giro this year, only the Tour', and managed to do so with the support of the Italian Cycling Federation.

When working as a courier in 1943-1944, Bartali was aware of the risks he took on every bicycle trip between Florence, Terontola, and Assisi. As if these risks weren't enough, he also hid a Jewish family at his home in Florence. Major Carità, the most ruthless of the collaborationists in Florence, held Gino prisoner for two days at his headquarters, known as the Villa Triste. When the Liberation came, Bartali ironically risked being shot by a group of resistance fighters between Tuscany and Lazio. One of them said he'd seen him pedalling dressed like a fascist (ie, wearing black). This was true, but it was an Italian postman's uniform, which Gino had used occasionally outside of Florence during his clandestine enterprises. Luckily, he was able to convince the resistance fighters who had interrogated him. Later, in 1948, he was also able to convince the journalist Gianni Brera, who had written an article in *La Gazzetta* stating that he was too old to win the Tour de France that year. He told me about this episode by saying: 'I took the train early one morning without telling Brera, and when I arrived at *La Gazzetta*'s editorial office he was amazed to see me. On his desk was a packet of Gauloises, without filters. I smoked five or six in an hour and said, "Do you still think I'm too old for the Tour?" Brera replied, "No, go ahead and good luck". Brera was a good writer, but he preferred Coppi, as did Fossati and almost all of the journalists at the time.'

Following the Giro d'Italia in the car with him, I never heard him utter a bad word once, rather like the phrases children learn today in kindergarten. He would say very nice little insults as much as possible. Paolo Conte wrote a magical song about him, about which Gino had only one reservation: 'It's a shame there are a few naughty words in the lyrics'. He continued, still on the subject of the song, to say: 'Maybe I do have a sad nose like a steep climb [see page 118], but Paolo Conte's nose is also very particular.'

This is the likeable, grouchy, Bartali, whose most famous saying was: 'It's all wrong. Do it all again!' It wasn't all wrong, because in his time (and even today), lots of things were wrong.

Gino followed the Ten Commandments and loved his neighbour, meaning he did what he considered right. It's no coincidence that today a tree is dedicated to him in the Garden of the Righteous Among the Nations (at Yad Vashem). Righteous with a capital R.

I think Bartali was stronger than Coppi (and I'm aware of offending several people by saying so). The latter had more style and elegance, but he was physically more fragile. Bartali was stronger, mentally as well as physically. He pedalled at a bit of an angle, but had an extraordinary energy which he attributed to his faith, and which certainly didn't come from doping. 'I tried once and fell asleep,' he said.

This book, and the story of one man cycling against the world, reminds us of one thing: when we're confronted with profound injustices, when rights and freedoms are flouted, when we witness atrocities such those carried out by the Nazi-fascists, it's right to rebel. Bartali knew this, long before Sartre wrote about it.

Gianni Mura
Italian journalist and writer

Endnotes

1. Medaglia d'oro al merito civile della Repubblica italiana.
2. 'Collaborò con una struttura clandestina che diede ospitalità ed assistenza ai perseguitati politici e a quanti sfuggirono ai rastrellamenti nazifascisti in Toscana, riuscendo a salvare circa 800 cittadini ebrei.'
3. 'Io non sopporto le prepotenze e i prepotenti.'
4. 'O la trovi subito o nun la trovi più.'
5. 'A' Ri, recordate de portà la bicicletta.'
6. 'Eravamo gente di campagna, figli di contadini!'
7. 'Cussì i pol magnar calcossa!'
8. 'Ero un pignolo della bicicletta. Quando mi mettevo in sella ero una cosa unica con lei. Non c'era un rumore, una vite fuori posto. La curavo da me. Tutto ciò che si sentiva quando andavo era il fruscio dell'aria attraverso i raggi delle ruote e quello dei tubolari sulla strada. Come ci tenevo alla bici ! Era la mia compagna, la mia vita, il mio strumento di lavoro!'
9. 'Era buono di carattere e aveva una specie di maschera di durezza dietro la quale si nascondeva.'
10. 'honteux et confus jura, mais un peu tard, qu'on ne le reprendrait plus'. Taken from the last two lines of the poem, Le corbeau et le renard, by Jean de la Fontaine.
11. 'Il 14 giugno 1936 accadde la cosa più tremenda della mia vita', Gino Bartali, *La mia storia*, Éditions La Gazzetta dello Sport, Milan, 1958.

12. A title given to saints who have been recognised as having made a significant contribution to theology or doctrine through their writing, research and study.

13. The seat of the Italian Chamber of Deputies

14. 'La X Olimpiade ha consacrato e rivelato al mondo i progressi dello sport italiano rigenerato dal fascismo e il valore degli atleti azzurri.'

15. 'Le ali dell'Italia fascista al comando di Balbo si impongono all'ammirazione del mondo vincendo l'Atlantico con un rapido e serrato volo.'

16. 'Binda, tre volte campione del mondo, ha conquistato brillantemente al traguardo dell'Arena la quinta vittoria nel Giro d'Italia aggiudicandosi il primo altissimo Premio del Duce e il primo premio del Direttorio del Partito.'

17. 'Bartali ha trionfato nel XXIV Giro d'Italia aggiudicandosi il 1° Premio del Duce.'

18. Baron Pierre de Coubertin was the founder of the International Olympic Committee and is often known as the father of the modern Olympics.

19. An Alpine mountain pass.

20. Apoteosi dello sport fascista nello stadio di Parigi. Strepitosa vittoria della squadra italiana nel campionato mondiale di calcio.

21. Da un traguardo all'altro nel ritmo incessante dei trionfi dello sport fascista.

22. Gruppi di connazionali, provenienti da centri vicini e lontani della Francia, sono saliti sulle montagne per incoraggiare ed acclamare Gino Bartali che passava dominando trionfalmente tutti gli avversari.

23. Quando Bartali correva, c'erano sempre centinaia di italiani che venivano a vederlo per loro era un dio. Quando lo vedevo in mezzo agli italiani, che lo veneravano e lo

celebravano, mi chiedevo come si potesse essere così amati.

24. The daily newspaper of the Vatican City State which reports on the activities of the Holy See and events taking place in the Church and around the world.

25. 'Il Papa è partito per Castel Gandolfo. L'aria dei Castelli Romani gli fa molto bene alla salute.'

26. 'Le razze umane esistono. Il concetto di razza è concetto puramente biologico. La popolazione dell'Italia attuale è nella maggioranza di origine ariana e la sua civiltà ariana. Esiste ormai una pura "razza italiana". È tempo che gli Italiani si proclamino francamente razzisti. Gli ebrei non appartengono alla razza italiana.'

27. 'Nei riguardi della politica interna, il problema di scottante attualità è quello razziale. E' in relazione con la conquista dell'impero, poiché la storia ci dimostra che gli imperi si conquistano con le armi, ma si tengono col prestigio. E per il prestigio occorre una chiara, severa coscienza razziale, che stabilisca non soltanto delle differenze, ma delle superiorità nettissime. Il problema ebraico è dunque un aspetto di questo fenomeno.'

28. Sono, benché ebrea, da lunghi secoli e più, italiana. Vedova. Mio marito fu ufficiale di fanteria, ferito e decorato nella Grande Guerra. Ho un unico figlio, iscritto al Politecnico. Sono da ben ventisei anni insegnante elementare con lodevole servizio. A me si toglie l'impiego necessario, a mio figlio la possibilità di studiare. Può essere che Voi riteniate meritato un simile spaventoso troncamento della nostra vita di perfetti italiani, nella nostra Italia ? Con fede ancora in Voi solo. Ossequio. Elvira Finzi.

29. 'Un'ora, segnata dal destino, batte nel cielo della nostra patria. L'ora delle decisioni irrevocabili.'

30. L'interrogatorio avvenne nel sottosuolo, presenti il maggiore Carità e altri tre militi. Un luogo sinistro, che incuteva terrore. Chi finiva là dentro non sapeva come sarebbe uscito. Mentre mi interrogava con tono inquisitorio e arrogante, il maggiore bestemmiava di continuo per offendermi e provocarmi. Sul tavolo vidi alcune lettere col timbro del Vaticano

31. Dovevo ricominciare da capo. … Mi viene in mente che molti, amici e avversari, cominciarono a chiamarmi il vecchiaccio.

32. Potevo ancora dimostrare a una generazione di giovani che non ero il nonno da portare a spasso di tanto in tante.

33. Andate, prodi corridori della corsa terrena e della corsa eterna!

34. La 'corsa del popolo' nella sua fulgida giornata di passione – Il delirante abbraccio dei triestini accoglie il Giro d'Italia.

35. Nuovo trionfo di Fausto Coppi che giunge solo al traguardo fiorito e luminoso di Sanremo.

36. Spettacolare fuga di Fausto Coppi sul Falzarego e sul Pordoi coperti di neve dopo un emozionante duello con Gino Bartali.

37. An Italian singer, pianist and composer.

38. The Guelfes and Gibelins were factions that supported the Pope and the Holy Roman Emperor, respectively, in the Italian city-sates of northern and central Italy.

39. Fictional characters created by the Italian writer and journalist Giovannino Guareschi. Don Camillo is the hot-headed priest of an Italian town, who is continuously at odds with the communist mayor, Peppone.

40. Avevamo soprattutto paura l'uno dell'altro e forse anche delle nostre ombre.

41. In Italian, the slogan rhymed: 'Brodo per campioni con dadi Arrigoni'.

42. 'Io sono sempre all'inseguimento di qualcosa'.

43. 'Io voglio essere ricordato per le mie imprese sportive e non come un eroe di guerra. Gli eroi sono altri. Quelli che hanno patito nelle membra, nelle menti, negli affetti. Io mi sono limitato a fare ciò che sapevo meglio fare. Andare in bicicletta. Il bene va fatto, ma non bisogna dirlo. Se viene detto non ha più valore perché è segno che uno vuol trarre della pubblicità dalle sofferenze altrui. Queste sono medaglie che si appuntano sull'anima e varranno nel Regno dei Cieli, non su questa terra.'